THE BAR COUNCIL OF ENGLAND AND WALES' INTERNATIONAL RULE OF LAW LECTURES – THE FIRST TEN YEARS

THE BAR COUNCIL OF ENGLAND AND WALES' INTERNATIONAL RULE OF LAW LECTURES – THE FIRST TEN YEARS

London
Wildy, Simmonds & Hill, Publishers

Bar Council of England and Wales' International Rule of Law Lectures: The First Ten Years

British Library Cataloguing-in-Publication Data:
A catalogue record for this book is available from The British Library

ISBN 9780854902125

Wildy, Simmonds & Hill Publishing

58 Carey Street

London WC2A 2JF

England

www.wildy.com

Printed in Great Britain

BAR COUNCIL OF ENGLAND AND WALES'
INTERNATIONAL RULE OF LAW LECTURES
THE FIRST TEN YEARS

CONTENTS

Preface

This book marks and celebrates 10 years of the Bar Council of England and Wales' International Rule of Law Lectures. The lecture series aims to stimulate debate, to inspire lawyers to participate in rule of law related work and to promote greater awareness of the importance of the rule of law. We have been fortunate over the past decade to attract outstanding speakers from across the globe, each with their own perspective on the rule of law and each with their own thoughts on the challenges presented.

We do not suggest that this collection is in anyway a complete reflection of the challenges that the rule of law has faced around the world during this period or, indeed, will face going forward. Each region and each age will face its own particular challenges. However, this collection of ten essays is very thought provoking and interesting. As a collection, it offers an insight into contrasting challenges faced around the world. In so doing, the collection reminds us that none of us should take for granted the existence of a functioning, transparent justice system with qualified and independent judges and lawyers.

It is perhaps fitting that the bookends of the first ten years are occupied by lectures on international courts, albeit very different ones. In 2007 the then President of the International Criminal Court, Justice Philippe Kirsch OC QC, kicked off this lecture series with a talk on the creation of the International Criminal Court over some fifty years and the establishment of accountability for the most serious international crimes. It was, as he acknowledged, a historic achievement. It is sobering that in 2016, ten years later, we are faced with South Africa starting the process of withdrawal from the court. This year's speaker, Baroness Françoise Tulkens, is a former Judge and Vice-President of a different international court, the European Court of Human Rights. Her talk, topical and thought-provoking, addresses "Fundamental Human Rights and State Security: Inseparable Allies".

The second and third lectures focused on the African experience. Judge Johann Kriegler, a former judge of the Constitutional Court of South Africa, gave a wide-ranging talk focusing, in the context of a number of former British colonies in Africa, on the right of individual citizens to participate in government, through regular, free and fair elections and to enforce those rights and other entitlements by means of accessible competent and independent courts. He finished on a positive note, commenting that the rule of law enjoys universal recognition as an aspirational norm and a benchmark of participatory democracy. The third lecture, by the Honourable Justice Anthony Gubbay, the former Chief Justice of Zimbabwe's Supreme Court, covered the progressive erosion of the rule of law in independent Zimbabwe. He spoke of a continuing struggle for the rule of law, which, among other things means, he said, the emancipation of the spirit of humankind from coercive constraints of fear, inequality and want. That struggle remains.

The fourth talk, "Justice in a Secularising and Pluralising Society", was given by the Archbishop of York, The Most Reverend and Rt. Hon. Dr. John Sentamu. This stimulating lecture addressed the increasing division, in the Archbishop's words, between what is legal on the one hand and what is moral on the other and the challenge which this diversion poses to law makers but, also importantly, to wider society.

Patricia O'Brien, the then Under-Secretary for Legal Affairs at the United Nations, in the fifth lecture, gave an informative talk covering a number of the legal issues facing the UN, including targeted sanctions, piracy and residual mechanisms. She was clear that the principle that everyone is accountable to the law, whether the individual or the State, is a fundamental concept driving much of the UN's work.

The 2012 lecture was given by Mark Mulholland QC, the then Chairman of the Bar of Northern Ireland. He gave a powerful talk on the rule of law and global terrorism, providing a Northern Irish perspective on this continuing international problem and concluding that the transition from conflict to conciliation, the world over, is made that much easier in a system where the rule of law has been respected.

The Chief Justice of Canada, the Right Honourable Beverley McLachlin PC, took as her theme, openness and the rule of law in 2014. While most would agree with Justice Brandeis that sunshine is one of the best disinfectants, she addressed the real tensions between open justice on the one hand and privacy and security on the other. She looked at how the courts can balance the open justice principle against countervailing interests of privacy and security, looking at where and when the line should be drawn.

The eighth talk was given by His Excellency Awn Al-Khasawneh, a former Vice President of the International Criminal Court and a former Prime Minister of Jordan, who provided a Middle Eastern perspective on the rule of law in turbulent times, focusing on the essential cultural unity of the region. His conclusion was hopeful, namely, that the region would find an inspiration to walk back from the abyss in its past history, past cosmopolitanism and in its ability to rise again after disasters.

In 2015, the ninth talk was given by the Honourable Chief Justice Ma of Hong Kong, "Strength and Fragility in Tandem: the Rule of Law in Hong Kong". Considering six indicators he concludes that although he hopes Hong Kong has passed the test, it is for the public to decide. Perhaps most pertinently for this series of lectures, Chief Justice Ma noted that it was healthy to have discussions and debates over the important topic of the rule of law – the price for enjoying the rule of law is eternal vigilance.

In 2016 looking around the world, and closer to home, I would agree, eternal vigilance is our job as lawyers, judges and people committed to maintaining the rule of law. Finally, I would like to thank the Bar Council for all their hard work in organising these lectures and this book, in particular Christian Wisskirchen and Jessica Crofts-Lawrence.

November 2016
Chantal-Aimée Doerries QC
Chairman of the Bar of England and Wales

The International Criminal Court: Establishing Accountability for the Most Serious International Crimes

JUDGE PHILIPPE KIRSCH

President of the International Criminal Court

19 February 2007

I am very pleased to be here this evening and would like to thank the Bar Council for the opportunity to speak with you about the International Criminal Court.

The Court greatly appreciates the support it has received from the Bar Council, both in terms of the Court's establishment and its development into an effective, independent legal institution. The Bar Council has assisted, for example, in the development of structures to support counsel appearing before the Court and has made a significant contribution to the development of the Code of Professional Conduct for counsel. Of course I would also be very pleased to see some of the Bar Council's members acting as counsel in future Court proceedings.

I will focus my remarks about the Court in four parts: the Court's creation; the features of the Court; the Court today; and what we should expect from the Court in the future.

The creation of the International Criminal Court was a process of over fifty years. The first responsibility for punishing genocide, crimes against humanity or war crimes, like any other serious crime, belongs to national legal systems. However, national courts were not always willing or able to act. Widespread or systematic violence all too often interfered with their willingness or ability to pursue justice. This may be because – as was the case in Nazi Germany, Cambodia, Rwanda – agents of the State themselves were complicit in or even directing the crimes. Or as we have seen in other situations, conflict can lead to the collapse of government structures, including the judiciary. In these situations, an international court is needed to punish serious crimes.

The international community realised very early on the need for an international court. This was the rationale for the Nuremberg and Tokyo Tribunals, established to punish offences committed during World War II. Despite these initial efforts, the onset of the cold war prevented the establishment of any other international criminal court for almost fifty years. During this time, serious crimes were committed around the world and went unpunished.

With the end of the cold war, the creation of an international criminal court became again a realistic possibility. However, the original trigger was not prosecution of genocide, crimes against humanity or war crimes, but a suggestion made to the United Nations General Assembly that an international criminal court be set up to deal with drug trafficking.

In the meantime, in the early 1990s, in response to more crimes on a massive scale in the former Yugoslavia and Rwanda, the United Nations Security Council established ad hoc tribunals for each of those countries. The ad hoc tribunals were pioneers and their functioning demonstrated two very important things. First, that international justice could work. Second, that these tribunals could not fulfil the role and need for a permanent international criminal court.

The tribunals suffered a number of inherent limitations which restricted their punishment and deterrent functions. First, such tribunals have only covered a particular country or geographical region. Crimes which occur elsewhere cannot be punished by these tribunals. Second, these tribunals respond primarily to events in the past. They are by and large not designed to address future crimes. Third, their creation depends on the political will of the international community of the day. As a result, such tribunals have been the exception, not the rule.

A permanent, international court was considered necessary to effectively respond to the most serious international crimes, and to overcome such limitations. In the summer of 1998, the UN General Assembly convened the Rome Conference to fill this essential need by establishing the ICC.

In creating the ICC, States were particularly concerned with guaranteeing the Court's underlying legitimacy. The Court is based on a very different foundation. Unlike the ad hoc tribunals, the ICC was created by an international treaty, enabling all States to participate in its creation. All States were invited to participate in the negotiations of the Statute, and the vast majority – 160 – did so. In negotiating the Statute, States sought wide agreement, without compromising the key values and objectives behind a fair and impartial court. Efforts towards universal acceptance were largely achieved, and on 17 July 1998, the Statute was approved by 120 States. One hundred and thirty-nine States signed the Statute before the deadline for signature expired at the end of 2000.

In just eight and a half years since the adoption of the Rome Statute, 104 countries – representing broad geographical diversity – have ratified or acceded to the Statute. This is a remarkable pace for a treaty establishing an international institution.

I would now like to turn to a number of key features of the Court.

I will start by defining the jurisdiction of the Court. The Court's jurisdiction is not universal. It is clearly limited to the most well-recognized bases of jurisdiction. The Court has jurisdiction over nationals of States Parties; or offences committed on the territory of a State Party.

In addition, the Court will have jurisdiction over situations referred by the Security Council in the exercise of its power to restore and maintain international peace and security. The Security Council can refer situations to the ICC independent of the nationality of the accused or the location of the crime. The Security Council has already used this power. In 2005, it referred the situation in Darfur, Sudan to the Court. The Security Council also has the power to defer an investigation or prosecution for one year in the interests of maintaining international peace and security.

The Court's jurisdiction is further limited temporally. The Court has jurisdiction only over events since its Statute entered into force on 1 July 2002.

The Court's subject matter jurisdiction covers the most serious international crimes. The ICC is not a human rights court. It has criminal jurisdiction over genocide, crimes against humanity, and war crimes. The Statute also provides that the Court has jurisdiction over the crime of aggression. However, the Court will not exercise this jurisdiction until both a definition of aggression and conditions for the exercise of jurisdiction are agreed upon. This must happen through an amendment to the Statute, agreed by the States Parties. Such amendment could occur at the earliest at a review conference to be held in 2009.

Even where the Court has jurisdiction, it will not necessarily act. The ICC is a court of last resort, intended to act where national courts are unwilling or unable. This is known as the "principle of complementarity." Under this principle, a case will be inadmissible if it is being or has been investigated or prosecuted by a State with jurisdiction. There is an exception for when the State is unwilling or unable genuinely to carry out the investigation or prosecution. For example, if the proceedings were undertaken solely to shield the person from criminal responsibility, or if the proceedings were carried out in a manner inconsistent with an intent to bring the person to justice. In addition, a case will be inadmissible if it is not of sufficient gravity to justify action by the Court. States and the accused have the right to challenge the admissibility of a case.

The guarantee of a fair trial and protection of the rights of the accused have paramount importance before the ICC. The Statute incorporates the fundamental provisions on the rights of the accused and due process common to national and international legal systems.

Subject to the requirements of the rights of the accused and the guarantee of a fair trial, victims are substantially integrated into the Court's proceedings. Victims may participate in proceedings even when not called as witnesses. The Court also has the power to order reparations to victims – including restitution, compensation, and rehabilitation. The need to take into account the particular interests of victims of violence against women and children is also specifically built into the Statute.

I would like to turn next to the Court today and give a brief overview of the Court's judicial and operational activities and related developments. I would note, first of all, that the jurisdiction of the Court can be triggered in three ways. First, a State Party may refer a situation alleging crimes committed by a national of or on the territory of a State Party. Second, the UN Security Council may refer a situation, independent of the nationality of the perpetrator or the location of the crimes. Third, the Prosecutor may begin an investigation on his own initiative or "proprio motu" into crimes committed on the territory of or by a national of a State Party. He may do so on the basis of information received from any credible source.

Three States Parties have referred situations occurring on their territories to the Court. In addition, as I already mentioned, the Security Council has referred the situation in Darfur, Sudan – a non-State Party.

Apart from the above situations, the Prosecutor has received over 2400 communications from various sources, primarily from individuals and nongovernmental organisations. The vast majority of these were dismissed as manifestly outside the jurisdiction of the Court – for example they allege crimes not within the Court's Statute or dealing only with non-State Parties. On the basis of the information received, the Prosecutor is monitoring five additional situations, only two of which he has made public: Côte d'Ivoire and the Central African Republic.

Last March, the first wanted person was surrendered to the Court. Mr. Thomas Lubanga Dyilo, a national of the Democratic Republic of the Congo, is alleged to have committed war crimes, namely conscripting and enlisting children under the age of fifteen years and using them to participate actively in hostilities. At the end of January, the judges of a Pre-Trial Chamber confirmed the charges against Mr. Lubanga. This decision has since been appealed. Should the Appeals Chamber uphold the confirmation of charges, the Court's first trial will start this year.

The Court has issued arrest warrants in the situation in northern Uganda for five members of the Lord's Resistance Army (LRA), including its leader Joseph Kony. One of the five individuals is now deceased. The other four warrants remain outstanding. The alleged crimes against humanity and war crimes contained in the warrants include sexual enslavement, rape, intentionally attacking civilians, and the forced enlistment of child soldiers.

The first Pre-Trial proceedings have been also been conducted in the situation in Darfur, Sudan dealing with issues such as the protection of victims and the preservation of evidence. The Prosecutor announced in December that his Office has collected enough evidence to identify some of those who bear the greatest responsibility for the worst crimes committed in Darfur. He stated that before presenting his evidence to the judges, he would assess whether the Government of the Sudan is conducting or has conducted genuine national proceedings concerning the same incidents and individuals that his investigation has identified.

The United Kingdom has a long history of judicial interpretation. By contrast, judges at the ICC are for the first time interpreting the provisions adopted in the Rome Statute. In the conduct of proceedings, they are addressing fundamental issues which will determine how future proceedings will be handled including, for example, the modalities of victims' participation in proceedings and disclosure of evidence. The Pre-Trial and Appeals Chambers have been dealing with these and other issues.

The Court's judicial activities are supported by its operational activities in the field. In addition to investigations, the Court carries out critical functions through its field operations including facilitating victims' applications for participation and reparations, protecting and relocating witnesses, supporting defence counsel, and conducting outreach to local populations.

The ICC operates in circumstances very different from any other court or tribunal. The Court is active in situations of ongoing conflict, where crimes continue to be committed. Security in the field continues to be an omnipresent concern. Our activities must be carried out in such a way as to ensure the safety of staff, victims, witnesses and others at risk.

I would like to turn now to what we can expect from the Court – and from this wider system of international justice – in the future. The Court's needs in the future flow from what I have already noted such as support for its field operations, arrest and surrender of wanted persons and security for its operations.

In establishing the ICC, States set up a system designed on two pillars. The Court itself is the judicial pillar. The enforcement pillar belongs to States. In national systems, the two pillars are intertwined. Courts rely automatically on the enforcement powers of the State. In the case of the ICC, the two have been separated. The Court depends on the cooperation of States.

The outstanding arrest warrants highlight just how essential this cooperation is. The Court does not have the power to arrest these persons. That is the responsibility of States and other actors. Without arrests, there can be no trials.

There are many other ways in which States can provide support to the Court's efforts, including executing arrest warrants, providing evidence, and enforcing sentences of the convicted. Because the Court's jurisdiction is limited to the nationals and territory of States Parties, continued ratification of the Statute is essential to the Court having a truly global reach.

The support of the United Nations has also been particularly important to enabling the Court's activities, especially in the field. The United Nations peacekeeping mission in the Congo has notably provided logistical support to the Court, such as accommodation and transport.

In addition to the operational cooperation I have just outlined, the Court relies on more general support. This general support is a shared responsibility of States as well as other actors. Non-governmental organisations, for example, have played a large role in urging ratification of the Rome Statute; assisting States in developing legislation implementing the Statute; and disseminating information about and building awareness of the ICC.

I would note in this context the important role bar councils may play in relation to the Court. Ignorance is one of the biggest obstacles to the success of the Court. Often, opposition to the Court is based on misconceptions which can be easily avoided. I believe that the more people understand the Court, the more it will be accepted. In generating discussion of the Court, bar council members can contribute to a greater understanding of the role of the ICC and its activities. Bar councils also make a significant contribution when they encourage their members to enrol in the list of defence council before the Court, as does the Bar Council of England and Wales.

The creation of the ICC was a historic achievement, more than fifty years in the making. Its creation was only the beginning. The Court now stands as a permanent institution capable of punishing perpetrators of the worst offences known to humankind. As early as 2004, the former UN Secretary-General Kofi Annan stated that the Court was "already having an important impact by putting would-be violators on notice that impunity is not assured and serving as a catalyst for enacting national laws against the gravest international crimes." To be fully effective, we must continue our efforts to ensure that the Court has the support necessary to dispense justice as fairly and efficiently as possible.

The Rule of Law in Post-Colonial Africa: A British Legacy?

JOHANN KRIEGLER

Retired Judge of the Constitutional Court of South Africa

3 December 2008

Thank you for the invitation to give this lecture. It is both a great honour and an intimidating challenge. Your Bar is not only the foremost body of forensic legal practitioners in the world but also the legendary training ground for public speakers. Therefore the very opportunity to engage with your members and guests is an exciting prospect for me. To be afforded, in addition, a platform to raise matters of great moment to African lawyers is a bonus. And then, by signal good fortune, the Damian Green debacle erupts to provide a relevant backdrop for a discussion of the Rule of Law. The flurry of conflicting opinions this incident has spawned, each asserted with absolute con- fidence in its irresistible veracity, foreshadows the imminent trundling-out of the Rule of Law, requiring one to examine yet again the meaning and applicability of this 'principle of constitutional law'. But allow me the Schadenfreude of observing that a police raid on the parliamentary office of an opposition MP does appear on the face of it to be characteristic of my country 20 years ago rather than of the mother of parliaments ...

Of course I realise that the invitation and the honour it entails are mine in a representative capacity only, not personally. They acknowledge the part played by the South African Constitutional Court in protecting and advancing the Rule of Law in a transitional democracy. But my vicarious involvement does not imply that I am in some way a spokesman for my profession. On the contrary, I have no constituency and am beholden to no-one. I speak my own mind and can do so frankly, keeping no backdoor open. I am answerable only to my own conscience, though I remain committed to the values I undertook to uphold when I took office as a member of that Court. I still regard it as my duty to protect and promote the fundamental values on which we hope to build a new society in my country.

Certain further prefatory disclaimers are, I believe, necessary. First, I am no blind admirer of Britain's colonial institutions and heritage. I am an Afrikaner whose grandfather was killed in battle defending his country's independence against British imperialism. Subsequently his widow and children, including my father then two years old, were transported to a series of concentration camps hundreds of miles from their deserted hearth and home. British colonial rule in Africa was no unmitigated curse, however. It brought a number of benefits, one of which, the Rule of Law, forms our subject matter tonight.

This leads to the second disclaimer. Although I have lived my professional life with English legal textbooks and judicial precedents, I am no common law expert. I became more or less familiar with concepts of your system of law by application, not instinct. In the case of the Rule of Law, however, the process was relatively simple. Although I cut my legal teeth on the Institutes of Justinian and not the profundities of Professor Dicey, I readily related to the concept of an overarching legal norm that governs all relationships, obligations and rights in an ordered society. Indeed, this major inarticulate premise of the law was acknowledged and applied in my country more than a century ago.

But, and this is the third and last disclaimer, I relate to the Rule of Law not as a philosopher but as a journeyman judge. Paraphrasing Oliver Wendell Holmes, I claim that the stuff of the law is experience – and having spent half a century applying and latterly administering the law in one capacity or another in South Africa and further afield, I believe I can claim expertise in two fields vital to the Rule of Law: independent courts and elections. Therefore, although I am no jurisprudent, I think I can rightly say that on these two topics I have expert knowledge based on extensive experience and I intend using them as my yardsticks in discussing our topic.

Having disavowed any profound theoretical understanding of the law, it would be a waste of time for me to venture a definition of the Rule of Law. Google records more than eight-and-a-half million entries under this heading, three-quarters of a million of them relating to the Rule of Law in conjunction with South Africa, and I have no intention of sifting through that overburden in search of payable ore. The term has been debased by gross over- and misuse, often serving as the last refuge of political hypocrites and other sophists. Genuine legal academics and professional associations have exhaustively debated it for decades.

More importantly, barely two years ago Lord Bingham delivered a magisterial lecture on the topic and I readily adopt his description of the core of this elusive concept.[1] In principle I believe it means that all persons and authorities within the state, whether public or private, are bound by and entitled to the benefits of laws that have been publicly and prospectively promulgated and that are publicly administered by courts of law. In particular, every wielder of public power is constrained by the law to function strictly within the limits of the empowering instrument. For my purposes this definition suffices. With apologies and acknowledgement to Justice Potter Stewart,[2] I can recognise an infringement of the Rule of Law when I see it.

In what follows I shall focus on two aspects of the Rule of Law: the right of each individual citizen (i) to participate in government through regular, free and fair elections; and (ii) to enforce such right and all other entitlements by means of accessible, competent and independent courts. I shall briefly survey a number of former British colonies in Africa of which I have personal and recent experience. Although each of these countries presents fascinating material for a case-study in depth, time constraints oblige me to limit the survey to a brief overview.

Imagine the map of Africa and superimpose a large question-mark, starting with Sierra Leone on the bulge of West Africa. Then sweep the curve through Uganda, turn south- eastwards through Kenya, head down through Malawi and Zimbabwe and mark South Africa as the dot at the foot. More specifically I shall concentrate on Kenya and South Africa in this survey, not only because they are the centres of gravity in their respective regions and cast a shadow beyond their borders, but also because I have particularly up-to-date knowledge of both.

SIERRA LEONE

Sierra Leone need not detain us long. After its emergence from colonial rule in the early 1960s the fledgling state languished, even before it was plunged into bloodshed and unimaginable cruelty some 25 years later. An uneasy peace imposed by external force in the mid 1990s has been succeeded by relative quietude, and three general elections have been held. The first of these, in 1997, was administered virtually wholly with foreign resources and expertise and established a reasonably legitimate legislature and executive. The second, in 2002, was conducted to a substantial extent

[1] See "The Rule of Law", *Cambridge Law Journal*, 66(1), March 2007, pp. 67-85.

[2] who famously observed that although he might not be able to define pornography, he knew it when he saw it.

by Sierra Leoneans and was seen by all concerned, including the general body of foreign observers, to have been free and fair. It was subsequently discovered, however, that the integrity of the election had in truth been marred by widespread corruption of the process and ballot-stuffing across the political board. The third election, administered in 2007 by a reconstituted electoral management body under dynamic new leadership and guided by Ghanaian advice, was a creditable exercise and laid a sound foundation for legitimate government.

There have, however, been serious lapses in national security, governmental abuse of power still occurs and policing is rudimentary and ineffectual – even in Freetown, which is generally better served than the remoter hinterland. In the absence of elementary essential services such as potable water, rubbish- and sewage-disposal, electricity and trafficable roads, the quality of life for the vast majority of Sierra Leoneans is so abysmal that speaking of the Rule of Law verges on the obscene. When last I was there, the only court really functioning was the International Criminal Court. Its acres of trim compound, neat and air-conditioned office buildings and state-of-the-art glass and steel court building stood in stark contrast to its shanty-town surroundings and the dilapidated local court buildings. Graham Greene's cotton trees and Levantine businessmen are still there, but Greene would hardly recognise the place – and of a useful colonial legacy pitifully little remains but some run-down colonial-era administration buildings. The prospects for the immediate future are not encouraging.

UGANDA

Let us proceed to Uganda, where President Yoweri Museveni restored a large measure of peace and stability in 1986 and later led his country out of the miasma into which Amin et al had plunged it. Despite a festering civil war, Museveni governed fairly benignly and his government, prodded from abroad, initiated commendable constitutional reforms during the 1990s. These were aimed at relaxing the tight one-party control that Museveni's National Resistance Movement had maintained since its victorious emergence from the bush. Although the implementation of these reforms was slow and accompanied by constitutional tension between the government and the judiciary, some progress was made towards multi-party democracy. But, at the same time, the security situation – which certainly is an ongoing cause of concern in the region – was proffered as justification for persistent governmental breaches of the Rule of Law, such as civilians being tried by courts martial for civilian crimes, leading to drum-head justice, double jeopardy, arrests without warrant and indefinite incarceration in secret places of detention.[3] The government did, however, acknowledge a general commitment to the Rule of Law.

Fairly recently, however, with the emergence of the president's former personal physician, Dr Kizza Besigye, as a presidential aspirant, a number of more retrograde steps have ensued. In November 2005, in the run-up to presidential elections, a large body of paramilitary men, officially styled the Joint Anti-Terrorist Team ('JATT') but more colourfully called the Black Mambas,[4] invaded the High Court building to block the release on bail of Besigye and 22 others who had been arrested some time before. The presiding judge was sufficiently intimidated to resign from the Bench shortly afterwards. The elections went ahead peacefully enough and the incumbent president and his party were re-elected with a comfortable plurality.

In March 2007 a large body of armed men in uniform again invaded the court building to block the judiciary in the exercise of its duties. This led to the International Bar Association's Human Rights Institute commissioning an enquiry by a delegation that I was privileged to lead. Our report records a disturbing number of serious breaches of the Rule of Law over and above those already mentioned, more particularly public criticism and veiled threats directed at individual judges by senior politicians, including the president himself, following rulings against the government; under-funding and under- staffing of the judiciary; repeated government defiance of court orders; and state harassment of opposition politicians, using the criminal justice system.[5]

On balance, however, matters could be much worse in Uganda. More specifically, although the Rule of Law may be honoured more in the breach than the observance, government does appear to be aware of the principle and to be embarrassed by the breaches. The most propitious portent, however, is that the judiciary is standing firm. The judges whom the IBA delegation met were not intimidated by the bully-boy tactics employed by the Black Mambas and their masters, rather the opposite. I came away heartened by the competence, dedication and courage of these men and

[3] These secret places of detention (and, reportedly, worse) are, with delightful irony, called 'safe houses'.

[4] The black mamba is a notoriously venomous and aggressive snake known in most of sub-Saharan Africa.

[5] The report Judicial independence undermined: A report on Uganda, an International Bar Association Human Rights Institute report (September 2007), details widespread inroads into the Rule of Law.

women. If in future they need support, the organised international legal profession should seriously consider renewing its earlier efforts.

KENYA

Let us then look at Kenya, the economic engine-room of East Africa – if Kenya sneezes the Great Lakes region takes to its bed with a raging fever. Kenya is a functioning multi- party democracy with a vigorous free-market economy, served competently by a vibrant and creative media sector. It has a wonderful climate sustaining rich agricultural farming and some of the world's most breathtaking scenery and wildlife. Approximately 77% of its 34 million people are said to be literate, its economy is healthy enough and the armed forces are substantially apolitical. It has a rich diversity of cultures and there is little, if any, religious animosity.

But this glowing picture is misleading. In the opening weeks of 2008 Kenya was rocked by widespread violence following general elections on 27 December 2007. The presidential election was claimed to have been stolen by the incumbent, President Mwai Kibaki, with the active connivance of the electoral management body. Some 1 200 people were killed, most of them in the northern Rift Valley where ethnic mixing and tension is comparatively high. Over 300 000 men, women and children were forced to flee their homes and livelihoods and many of them are still in tented refugee camps, possibly never to return home. The main opposition, the Orange Democratic Movement, and its presidential candidate, Raila Odinga, refused to accept the presidential election result, Kibaki stood his ground and the country was plunged into a constitutional crisis, hamstringing the economy of the whole region.

The African Union intervened, a mediation panel of eminent Africans, led by former UN Secretary General Kofi Annan, was mustered and eventually an uneasy settlement was brokered. One of the terms of the deal was the appointment of a commission of enquiry to investigate all aspects of the elections, including the integrity of the presidential result, and to recommend improvements to the electoral system and its legal framework. This commission, which I chaired, conducted a six-month investigation in the course of which we scrutinised electoral material, interrogated electoral officials, held specialist workshops, reviewed academic material, criss-crossed the country hearing over a thousand interlocutors, subjected a number of key witnesses to cross-examination by our own counsel and by advocates acting on behalf of the interested parties in a quasi-adversarial process, and eventually produced a report.[6]

Although the investigation was directed towards the elections, much of what relates to our topic can be gleaned from this report. I can and should, however, add some observations that are pertinent in the present context. The commission was, for instance, not mandated to review the competence of the Kenyan judiciary or the suitability of its procedures. Yet, in the course of the enquiry, especially in relation to the examination of the electoral dispute mechanisms available to disgruntled candidates in Kenyan law and practice, it became apparent that there were serious shortcomings, of substance, procedure and, regrettably, of attitude.

An election petition is inherently urgent and, albeit indirectly, affects the interests of tens of thousands of voters in addition to the candidates and political parties. In the case of a presidential election and in some instances in national legislative elections, the result could determine the identity of the national government. Speedy, appropriate and effective remedies are of paramount importance.

Moreover, all election cases are highly contentious and excite public emotion. Consequently the traditional prophylactic function of court proceedings is extremely important; and, of course, the educative function of the judicial process is also of particular importance when there are so many interested onlookers. Therefore election cases should be handled with the utmost care and expedition. Yet a number of the barrage of electoral cases lodged in the wake of the disputed elections were still unresolved more than eight months after the announcement of the election results.[7] I was struck more than once by a predilection to focus on the procedural niceties so beloved of lawyers and hated by the lay public – for instance, was there or was there not proper and/or timely service of the petition on the successful candidate? If not, did the substituted service comply with the prescribed requirements? These peripheral issues were more often than not determined by oral hearings with lengthy cross-examination, followed by appeals – the whole elaborate paraphernalia of private law-suits – while

[6] The Report of the Independent Review Commission on the General Elections held in Kenya on 27th December, 2007, dated 17th September 2008, is available from the Government Printer, Nairobi, and, together with its supporting documents, on the Panel's website www.dialoguekenya.org.

[7] Although the Commission did not research the data, there was ample evidence from electoral administrators, informed journalists, legal practitioners and politicians that election petitions in Kenya have for many years been notoriously drawn-out affairs, occasionally remaining undecided when the next elections fall due.

the underlying political issues festered. I was especially horrified to see an election petition being dismissed on a preliminary point of standing years after the petition had been lodged.

The received wisdom seems to be that the procedural rules for the initiation of an electoral complaint were not only devised and imposed by the Medes and Persians but are to be followed with the precision of an ophthalmic surgeon. The time-honoured techniques employed by judicial officers and practitioners to kick for touch and the little stratagems they use to disguise their dilatory intentions are universal, at least in the English-speaking world. They are alive and well in Kenya.

The Kenyan judiciary has from time to time been severely criticised and on occasion subjected to mass purges on the grounds of its corruption, real or perceived. Its image is tainted. Obviously there are exceptions but the judiciary as a whole seems vulnerable to criticism and enjoys little media support. While I was in Kenya the judiciary sought to resist moves by the executive to impose quality control and performance-related contracts but this was generally seen – or at least represented by the media – as self-serving. The judges enjoyed no visible public support.[8] The potential impact of such measures on the independence of the judiciary and the importance of such independence for the protection of fundamental human rights was to the best of my knowledge never raised. If it was, it had no significant effect on the public debate. Judges were seen to be government functionaries who were obliged to fit in with standard control measures for civil servants. This attitude, to my mind, is irreconcilable with the role of judges in a polity where the Rule of Law prevails.

It goes without saying that independence does not mean unaccountability. Without doubt judges, who are paid from the public purse to serve their country and its people, are not free agents, privateers at liberty to do as they wish without being answerable for their actions (or, more often, lack thereof). But clearly judges should not be subject to the orders or supervision of bureaucrats or politicians. A judicial code of conduct, transparently and punctiliously applied by the judiciary, alone or with some outside participation, is the best remedy for judicial misconduct. Judges must do their work in public, giving the reasons for their rulings in public, and be subject to public correction by higher tribunals. If this elementary contention was put forward in the course of the Kenyan debate it eluded me.

[8] Indeed, the Law Society was agitating for the removal of the Chief Justice.

I was even more depressed by the poor standard of advocacy I encountered, always a reliable indicator of the quality of judicial proceedings in a jurisdiction. Just as much as a Bench is dependent on the quality of the input made by the Bar, so does a Bar grow or shrink in stature and competence to fit the Bench with which it interacts. Not only did some of the advocates with whom we worked not do their homework, they proved factually unreliable, by my lights an unforgivable deficiency that has to be firmly addressed and relentlessly stamped out. Once mutual trust between Bar and Bench is lost, the administration of justice suffers, the standard of adjudication drops and the Rule of Law falters.

The most significant feature of public life in Kenya reflecting on the state of the law and the sanctity of its Rule relates to the electoral process we had to evaluate. It became increasingly clear as our investigations progressed that there was no moral sanction against any kind of electoral skulduggery. Not even the eleventh commandment – 'Thou shalt not be caught out' – has any force. No-one can remember when last anybody was criminally prosecuted for an electoral offence. Vote-buying, bribery, ballot-stuffing, impersonation, intimidation – anything goes and everybody accepts it as normal, natural, satisfying and right.

There are standard rates for vote-buying and standard methods for its perfection. For the benefit of illiterate, paralysed or similarly incapacitated voters there is a procedure whereby one can ask that a 'friend' assist one to cast one's vote; and if one has sold one's vote, the buyer ensures delivery by providing the 'friend'. Although more than three- quarters of the Kenyan population are said to be literate, we had it on no less an authority than that of a member of the electoral management body that roughly 70% of voters were 'assisted'. Accepting that the electoral commissioner in question was exaggerating, it was still common cause that vast numbers of voters adopted this fraudulent stratagem.

No-one, not a single voter, not one politician, academic, journalist or lawyer, not even an electoral administrator, ever made the point that the practice of vote-buying denied the voters concerned their inalienable right to participate in their governance. No-one gave a passing thought to this right for which men and women had fought and died for so long. Nor did it seem to upset anybody that this denial of the citizens' right to have a say in their government assailed their essential humanity. It was also quite clear that at least the two main competing parties in the presidential race resorted to ballot-stuffing on an industrial scale in polling stations where there were no opposition agents present. Turnout percentages that would have been the envy of Mr Stalin were recorded and accepted without demur, I suspect on the revered principle of tit for tat. Participatory democracy is really not seen as an element of the Rule of Law in Kenyan politics.

Hardly less disturbing is the circumstance that not a single one of the many thousands of electoral observers regarded this pandemic of electoral fraud as sufficiently important to note. Many well-meaning and principled human rights activists, many skilled and disinterested foreign observers, some of them British, made nothing of these features.[9] To anyone who respects the truth, who respects the Rule of Law, this wholesale condonation of the abandonment of electoral propriety and absolution for blatant transgressions is ominous. The Report accordingly impressed upon the Kenyan authorities that this prevailing spirit of electoral corruption was a root cause of the polluted Kenyan elections and the violence they triggered. The 2007 elections were indeed stolen, but not by a gang of conspirators from those who complained so vociferously; they were stolen from the people of Kenya by their political process.

Unless and until this major departure from the Rule of Law is frankly acknowledged and addressed, future elections augur ill for Kenya. The ever-present undercurrent of ethnic tension, the century-old unresolved land claims and the growing frustration of the unemployed underclass in the sprawling peri-urban shanty towns will continue to spill over in bloodshed as long as elections in Kenya remain the sham that they are.

Therefore, although there are significant vestiges of the British colonial legacy in Kenya, they are in need of refurbishing. Kenya itself is important and its role in relation to the region is even more significant. The human material is there but without assistance from beyond its borders, the country is unlikely to make the necessary reassessment or carry through with the necessary reforms.

[9] On the contrary, donor community representatives at first gave the 2007 elections their all but unqualified stamp of approval for all processes up to the point where the presidential votes were collated at the central data collation centre. When, many months later, I drew the attention of this august body of diplomatic representatives to the manifest and manifold shortcomings in the electoral process as a whole, starting with an inadequate and skewed register of voters and culminating in widespread abuse of the balloting process, I was met with disbelief and hostility. I suppose that in the circumstances I should not have been shocked when one particular mission, backed by prestigious academics, tried to pressure me personally to suppress certain evidence.

MALAWI

We can skip lightly through Malawi, not because it is small or unimportant but because there is at the moment no real cause for concern about Malawi and the Rule of Law. In a generally peaceful society, since Dr Hastings Banda was persuaded to retire some 16 years ago, multi-party elections have been held regularly and are largely uneventful. The real competition for political power is conducted by jockeying for majority alliances within parliament.

The judiciary and its independence have not been particularly contentious issues in recent times. Everybody has hopefully (!) learnt a lesson from a constitutional crisis that arose some years ago when the then Speaker and some colleagues resolved to bring some bright young high court judges down a peg or two and summoned them to appear before parliament. A low-key intervention by two senior lawyers from abroad seemed to have a beneficial effect. Latterly the independence of the Malawian judiciary seems to have reached calmer waters and the legal profession of this charming country can be left to putter on quietly. The country is gearing up for general elections next year. I expect to be involved in a consultative capacity in what augurs to be a successful process.

ZIMBABWE

You do not need me to tell you anything about that tragically failed state or the heroism of our friends and colleagues there. They, not Mugabe and the coterie of wicked men he has gathered around him, carry the spirit of Zimbabwe. They are the hope for the restoration of that once good and prosperous land: Beatrice Mtetwa, Sternford Moyo, Irene Petros, Arnold Tsunga, Joseph James, Josephat Tshuma, David Drury, Tino Bere, Mordecai Mahlangu – the roll of honour is too long to mention all. The illustrious list goes on and on: people who make me proud to call myself a lawyer; people who refuse to be cowed even in the face of police beating and arrest, who stick to their task and keep the torch of freedom under the law alive. Last Friday, 28 November 2008, they enjoyed a significant forensic victory. Judge Luis Mondlane, speaking on behalf of a Southern African Development Community Tribunal sitting in Windhoek, handed down judgment in the case of Campbell v Zimbabwe. The court ruled that the Zimbabwean government had violated its treaty obligations in denying Mr Campbell and other farmers access to the courts to seek protection of their property rights. The government was consequently ordered to 'take all measures to protect the possessions and ownership of the farmers'. Notwithstanding the government's defiant and contemptuous response, the judgment sounds a clear and ringing endorsement of the Rule of Law in Southern Africa. It also provides a basis on which to build once reconstruction can start in Zimbabwe. So, in these last days of the evil regime, we should be preparing our plans to speed that recovery.

Ironically, in this most benighted of Britain's one-time colonies in Africa, the legacy of that former era is the most noteworthy. The current judiciary might be hopelessly compromised and the proud tradition of Telford George, Enoch Dumbutshena and Tony Gubbay, who led the Zimbabwean judiciary with such distinction, besmirched by grubby collaborators, and the memory of decent elections might be overridden by Mugabe's shabby charades. Nevertheless belief in the inherent dignity and worth of human beings and the indispensable role of the Rule of Law in vouchsafing these values survives. The steadfastness of those preserving this grail is sure evidence that they are heirs to the spirit that kept Britain going in its finest hour.

SOUTH AFRICA

Lastly, my own country. Providing even the briefest of overviews of the current status of the Rule of Law in South Africa would require many hours. Providing sufficient political background and historical contextual material would require a whole series of lectures. I am therefore forced to give you a highly personalised perspective on what I regard as the most salient features.

Superficially we have retained much of the English judicial legacy. In practice our South African forensic style is firmly rooted in our British colonial heritage. You would, for instance, feel quite at home in our civil or criminal trial and appeal courts, where the procedure is English in origin and spirit, adversarial and litigant-driven, with 'm'luds', 'with respects', 'my learned friends', cross-examination, objections to leading questions or hearsay, and all the other robed and bibbed trappings so dear to the hearts of the tabloids and television. (We have, however, unlike many of our kindred jurisdictions in Africa, never taken to wigs).[10]

More substantively, we have for more than a century, even in the darkest days of apartheid, professed adherence to the Rule of Law. Many interested but uninformed observers have a fairly simple two-dimensional

[10] No-one who has sweated under a wig in a hot and humid courtroom would not applaud the perspicacity of our distant predecessors who declined to follow this practice in our courts.

perception of South Africa before 1994. They would be surprised to hear the ringing declarations of libertarian principle that occasionally fell from the lips of judges in those days and would not comprehend how Felicia Kentridge, Arthur Chaskalson and others in the Legal Resources Centre were able, by means of public interest litigation – that is, by using the courts – to chip away at the granite face of the regime. The uninformed observer would not be able to understand how, by these means, step by tiny yet inexorable step, the mighty influx control edifice, a vital component of 'grand apartheid', could be brought down.

But apartheid South Africa was not two-dimensional. It was infinitely more complex.[11] Much of that complexity remains. South Africa, nearly two decades after its emergence from apartheid, is still a very strange society and anybody who oversimplifies it will not be able to gain a real understanding of the country and its people. Clearly this is not the time or the place to provide a comprehensive description of present-day South Africa in all its fascinating complexity – even if I were capable of providing it. Broad background strokes relevant to our topic are all that we have time for.

Any discussion of the Rule of Law in South Africa must start with the Constitution, section 1 of which provides as follows:

> The Republic of South Africa is one sovereign democratic state founded on the following values:
>
> (a) Human dignity, the achievement of equality and the advancement of human rights and freedoms.
>
> (b) Non-racialism and non-sexism.
>
> (c) Supremacy of the constitution and the rule of law.
>
> (d) Universal adult suffrage, a national common voters roll, regular elections and a multi-party system of democratic government, to ensure accountability, responsiveness and openness.

[11] I have been impressed by a recent publication, Jens Meierhenrich's *The Legacies of Law, Long-Run Consequences of Legal Development in South Africa, 1652-2000* (Cambridge University Press, 2008), which grasps and seeks to explain the curious dichotomy of the law under apartheid, in part commendably liberal but also harshly discriminatory, normative and prerogative in the author's lexicon.

There is also no dispute about the formal independence of the judiciary and the duty of the government and all organs of state to protect it. Section 165 of the Constitution is unequivocal and unchallenged:

(1) The judicial authority of the Republic is vested in the courts.

(2) The courts are independent and subject only to the Constitution and the law, which they must apply impartially and without fear, favour or prejudice.

(3) No person or organ of state may interfere with the functioning of the courts. (4) Organs of state, through legislative and other measures, must assist and protect the courts to ensure the independence, impartiality, dignity, accessibility and effectiveness of the courts.

(5) An order or decision issued by a court binds all persons to whom and organs of state to which it applies.

One should not forget, however, that South Africa has but recently transmogrified from a neo-colonial racial oligarchy into a fully-fledged constitutional democracy based on freedom, equality and human dignity, separation of powers and express adherence to the Rule of Law. Our extensive and wholly justiciable Bill of Rights was therefore an enormous leap for humankind and a novelty for the country. In the last decade of the twentieth century South Africa produced a miracle. Very much to the surprise of the world and the delight of South Africans, the country's political leaders negotiated a bloodless revolution, averting a racial Armageddon and reversing a 350-year tradition of colonial and neo-colonial rule. But the country's transformation brought a multitude of problems, many foreseen yet unavoidable. These problems were daunting.

The judiciary is a vivid example. The decision to exchange apartheid for freedom and equality under a libertarian and egalitarian constitution, protected, interpreted and applied by an independent judiciary, was relatively straightforward and pain-free. Identifying and defining the fundamental rights to be enshrined in the Bill of Rights presented no insurmountable obstacles. Indeed, the main participants in the negotiation process at times seemed to vie with one another in articulating libertarian principles. There was also no noticeable opposition to wholehearted acceptance of the separation of powers doctrine. The problem lay with the practicalities. For instance, the existing staffing of the courts, especially the magistracy, was heavily biased in favour of white Afrikaner men and self-evidently there had to be adaptation, rapid and radical. The pale male face of the judiciary had to change so as to mirror more closely the society it was to serve. In the old South Africa, appointments to the high court Bench came all but invariably from the ranks of the senior Bar. Although Afrikaners were not predominant at the Bar, white men made up the bulk of the practising advocates in the country for many years. At the time of the transition to democracy, in South Africa as it then was there was one judge who was not male and one who was not white; in addition there were a number of female and black magistrates.

The influx of relatively large numbers of judicial officers from outside the former pool of experienced practitioners called for (and still requires) extraordinary measures to supplement the lack of experience of these newcomers. Manifestly this was an urgent necessity but unfortunately there was much dithering and pettifogging turf-protection about the establishment of a proper judicial education institute, an enterprise that I pursued more or less full-time at the invitation of the then Minister of Justice and Chief Justice after my retirement but eventually abandoned some years ago. Now, 15 years into the new South Africa, a statute has been adopted making provision for the creation of such a body. Heaven knows when it will be up and running and heaven knows what is happening to the standard of adjudication in the meantime.

There are a number of excellent but inexperienced men and women on the Bench who are unfairly expected to do the impossible. I can well remember how nervous and tentative I was when first I sat as a judge – and I had some 20 years of high court experience and umpteen battles behind me. There is a more ominous feature of judicial transformation in my country: latterly some rapidly promoted but insufficiently experienced persons, otherwise well qualified to undertake the work of a judge and with loads of promise, have proved unable to bear the heavy personal burdens that judicial office inevitably brings with it.[12] The result was predictable: aberrant judgments and questionable behaviour by judges have elicited sharp public criticism, a good deal of it, unfortunately, justified.

This has come at a most unpropitious time. The political scene in South Africa is in a state of flux. Mr Thabo Mbeki, the country's president since

[12] A particularly sad case in point is that of Judge John Hlophe, a highly gifted young man, potentially a fine jurist, who, having been appointed to the Cape Bench from academia at age 36 in 1995 and then elevated to Judge President of the Cape High Court in 2000, somehow lost the plot and became involved in a succession of distasteful public spats evidencing, in the main, his lack of judicial maturity. Several of these incidents have not only involved Hlophe JP in contention but reflected on the South African judiciary generally.

1999, was prematurely forced out of office in September this year by an extra-parliamentary resolution of the National Executive Committee of the ruling African National Congress (ANC). Thus the head of state was brought to his knees, not by an open vote of the national legislature for stated reasons but by the surreptitious manoeuvring of a political clique. For reasons that were not made known to the public, the ANC did not nominate its president, Mr Jacob Zuma, to replace Mr Mbeki but instead put forward Mr Kgalema Motlanthe, its deputy president, and he was duly elected by the National Assembly as interim president. I say 'interim' because the country is due to go to the polls at some time as yet unannounced but probably in the second quarter of 2009. Mr Motlanthe has replaced a number of the Mbeki cabinet appointees, some of whom have made public pronouncements suggesting that they regard their appointments as long-term. Certain current cabinet ministers are seen to be Zuma supporters while others are more likely to be neutral.

I mention these ostensibly irrelevant political features because they are indeed highly relevant to any prognosis on the Rule of Law in South Africa. The ANC, in alliance with two left-wing partners, the South African Communist Party and a trade union confederation known by its acronym COSATU, controls the political stage with a 70% majority in Parliament. This is sufficient to bring about virtually any constitutional amendment that it deems desirable. At the same time influential figures within the ANC alliance have been making ominous utterances about the judiciary, echoes of the 1980s when the ANC, still a revolutionary liberation movement in exile, was debating what it would do with the judiciary once it came to power. One school of thought was then strongly in favour of a radical purge. Happily for me and other serving judges a more conservative view prevailed.

But there are signs that the radicals are once again pushing for 're-education' and 'reorientation' of the judiciary. It has become quite common for some or other ANC spokesperson to commend or excoriate a judgment and/or its author depending on its perceived political effect. Recently even the judges of the Constitutional Court, the highest court in the land with an unchallenged track record of excellence since its formation in 1994, have been publicly accused of political manipulation, of pursuing a 'counter-revolutionary agenda' and of trying to block the ascent of Mr Zuma to the presidency.

Although I believe these foolish attempts to bend the judiciary to the political will of the ruling party will fail, one cannot be certain. Indeed, if some of the wilder rhetoric is to be taken seriously, there is an identifiable risk that someone within the ruling alliance might next year persuade the new government that some or all of the judges should be brought to heel. Although the venom has emanated from the usual suspects,[13] the new secretary general of the ANC has emerged as a prime broadcaster of unbridled attacks on the judiciary and individual judges apropos politically significant judgments that do not meet with his approval. (Not all of this revolutionary nonsense has come from politicians. Some startling judicial statements have been published, suggesting for example that the whole body of pre-1994 South African law, including our entire common law, should be scrapped as an unwanted relic of the racist past.)

These political developments must be seen against the backdrop of concerted efforts over a number of years by the Ministry of Justice and Constitutional Development to enact an array of statutory measures aimed at increasing executive control over the judiciary. To date the judiciary, to an extent assisted by the Bar, has managed to hold at bay the more egregious of these enactments but some have found their way onto the statute book and will have to be confronted sooner rather than later. And although the Minister of Justice and Constitutional Development newly appointed by President Motlanthe, Mr Enver Surty, has made some reassuring noises relating to the independence of the judiciary, neither he nor anyone else in government or within the upper echelons of the ruling ANC has seen fit publicly to repudiate their comrades who malign and ridicule judges. The Minister, who is after all the constitutional link between the judiciary and the other two pillars of state, has on no occasion protected the judges against their political detractors. No voice has been heard from the legislature or the executive in defence of the judiciary or its independence. Certainly no leading figure in the governing party has decried the attacks.

This is hardly surprising. The measures directed at bringing the judiciary to heel flow directly from resolutions adopted by the ANC in national conference some years ago that were substantially reiterated at last December's watershed ANC conference (where Mr Mbeki was dealt a humiliating defeat by Mr Zuma in the contest for the presidency of the party). Significantly, the prime mover behind the statutory encroachments, in a very real sense their author, parliamentary patron and executive champion, Mr Johnny de Lange, a determined ANC loyalist, has been retained as Deputy Minister of Justice and Constitutional Development. These moves have assumed sinister dimensions now that the ANC has

13 For example, ANC Youth League president Mr Julius Malema, a notorious source of wild and woolly utterances, and general secretary of the South African Communist Party Dr Blade Nzimande, who has been mentioned as a serious contender for the vice-presidency next year.

elected as its president – and therefore the presumptive national president – a man who has been and still is embroiled in prolonged criminal proceedings with the National Prosecuting Authority. This, sadly but inevitably, has brought the criminal justice system, and with it the judiciary, into the sights of the more ardent Zuma loyalists. The implications for the Rule of Law are all too plain.

Manifestly there is a need for a reasoned and rational defence of the South African judiciary, its integrity and its independence. The judiciary itself is constitutionally, traditionally and structurally incapable of entering the hustings on its own behalf or in defence of particular judges. The legal profession is not structured or organised to assume this task. Unfortunately neither is any other institution equipped – or, if equipped, willing – to speak publicly in defence of the judiciary and to warn of the imminent threat that attacks on the integrity and the competence of judges pose for the Rule of Law. Over and above the necessity of defending the judiciary against political attack, there is an urgent need to educate the public about the Rule of Law, to explain why the independence of the judiciary is important to each individual citizen, and to show how and why these apparently abstruse and remote matters are essential for the protection of individual rights and freedoms.

This message must be brought home to the people of the whole of the Southern African region. The crisis in Zimbabwe, tragic in itself, has revealed an even more tragic lack of vision on the part of the political leadership in the region, vision that will be indispensable once post-Mugabe reconstruction is to be undertaken in Zimbabwe. Concerted regional efforts will not be possible without an extensive public information campaign to sensitise the people to the importance of the basic values of the Rule of Law. (As matters stand right now, the average South African has little knowledge of or appreciation for these values. On the contrary, the recent eruptions of xenophobic violence throughout the country would rather suggest public support for the government's callous attitude towards these unhappy victims of events over which they have no control.)

The outlook may be gloomy but that is no reason to wallow in self-pity or despair. We in Southern Africa are not unfamiliar with threats to the independence of the judiciary and the concomitant erosion of the Rule of Law. We have held out before and will do so again. Over time and by dint of hard work, we will be able to generate sufficient public understanding of and support for the Rule of Law to reverse the current downward trend. Some of us have, as individuals, raised our voices, but with limited success. Often the message has been overlooked in the rush to stone the messenger.

We need a concerted effort with support spanning the spectrum of our diverse societies.

To this end, therefore, a number of us, concerned Southern African lawyers, have put aside our ideological and other differences to establish an organisation to promote democracy under law and to advance understanding of and respect for the Rule of Law in Southern Africa. Freedom Under Law was recently incorporated (in South Africa and Switzerland) as a not-for-profit entity committed to promoting democracy under law and advancing understanding of and respect for the Rule of Law. The board of directors, drawn from the legal profession in Southern Africa and chaired by myself, enjoys the patronage of a prestigious international advisory board chaired by the Rt Hon the Lord Steyn.[14]

To return then, on that positive note, to the question posed at the outset: Does anything of value remain of the Rule of Law in Britain's former colonies in Africa? The answer is in the affirmative, but not without qualification. The Rule of Law is indeed acknowledged throughout Anglophone Africa as a guiding principle of statecraft. It enjoys universal recognition as an aspirational norm, a benchmark of participatory democracy; and even though this is often mere lip service, it is nevertheless heartening.

[14] Those who would like more information about Freedom Under Law are welcome to communicate with me at johannkriegler@mweb.co.za.

The Progressive Erosion of the Rule of Law in Independent Zimbabwe

THE HONOURABLE JUSTICE ANTHONY R GUBBAY

Former Chief Justice of the Supreme Court of Zimbabwe

9 December 2009

When several months ago I received an invitation to deliver the third annual International Rule of Law lecture, I was not only surprised, but extremely delighted. It is an honour and a privilege for one whose career in the law began, and ended, in a country many thousands of miles away, whose system of law is founded on old Roman Dutch principles, to have been chosen to grace this auspicious occasion. Yet, it is an undeniable fact that whatever system of law is applicable, whether it is the English common law, the Napoleonic Code, my own, or that of other countries, the rule of law forms an essential foundation in any democratic system of governance. It is a concept of universal validity and application. It embraces those institutions and principles of justice which are considered minimal to the assurance of human rights, and the dignity of man.

Although there is a wide variety of jurisprudential thought on the complex concept of the rule of law, it is generally accepted that a society in which the rule of law prevails is one in which a climate of legality, observance of the law and an effective judiciary, are evident. It is a society in which no man is punishable, or can be made to suffer bodily or proprietary loss, except for a breach of the law as established by ordinary courts of the land. It does not mean the protection of vested interests, or unfair exploitation in society. It means the emancipation of the spirit of humankind from coercive constraints of fear, inequality and want. It requires that everyone should be subject to the law equally, and that no one should be above the law; that law enforcement agencies and the courts enforce and apply the law impartially.

The rule of law is the antithesis of the existence of wide, arbitrary and discretionary powers in the hands of the executive. It is a celebration of individual rights and liberties, and all the values of a constitutional democracy, characterized by the absence of unregulated executive or legislative power. It is a society in which the rule of law is observed, through the mechanism of judicial review. Executive decisions and legislative enactments, outside the framework of the law, are declared invalid, thereby compelling both the executive and the legislature to submit to enjoyment, by the individual, of all rights and liberties guaranteed by the constitution.

An independent judiciary and legal profession are critical elements of the rule of law. The bedrock of a constitutional democracy is an independent judiciary. A judiciary which is not independent from the executive and legislature renders the checks and balances inherent in the concept of separation of powers ineffective.

It is a matter of concern that during the eight year period preceding the recent formation of the coalition government in Zimbabwe, the avowed policy of the executive was to appoint as judges to both the Supreme and High Courts, persons known to be sympathetic to its political ideals. In this it has been successful. The Supreme Court soon lost four of its five judges, with its composition being increased to eight; it is now six. The High Court lost eight of its judges, most of who resigned in the face of personal adversity. The vast majority of all the judges, including the Chief Justice, perceiving the unending land invasions as a political and not a legal issue, have gratefully accepted free occupation of large tracts of the most productive agricultural land, expropriated from white commercial farmers. In so doing they have compromised their judicial independence, seemingly pre-judged the legality of the fast-track land programme and associated issues, and seriously breached the rule of law, which they are oath bound to protect and enforce.

Moreover, about two years ago, it was widely reported that the Reserve Bank of Zimbabwe had supplied judges with flat screen television sets, satellite decoders and generators, at no charge. A payment or perquisite accepted by a judge from any source other than the treasury, inevitably raises the taint of undue influence. (Political interference with the judiciary was confirmed in the 2004 report to the International Council of Advocates and Barristers, entitled 'The State of Justice in Zimbabwe', by a team of eminent jurists, chaired by Stephen Irwin QC).

The Constitution of Zimbabwe places particular significance on the rule of law, specifically in the context of Chapter III rights. So, for instance, the rule of law is encapsulated in the preamble to the Declaration of Rights. Section eleven, which constitutes the 'the key or umbrella provision' of Chapter III, provides:

> 'Whereas persons in Zimbabwe are entitled, subject to the provisions of this Constitution, to the fundamental rights and freedoms of the individual specified in this Chapter, and whereas it is the duty of every person to respect and abide by the Constitution and the laws of Zimbabwe, the provisions of the Chapter shall have effect for the purpose of affording protection of those rights and freedoms subject to such limitations on that protection as are contained herein, being limitations designed to ensure that the enjoyment of the said rights and freedoms by any person does not prejudice the public interest or the rights and freedoms of other persons'.

This means that conduct negatively impacting on the constitutional rights of an individual may only be embarked upon in so far as such impacting is constitutionally permitted, and subject to the Constitution and other laws of Zimbabwe. Conduct that infringes constitutional rights, but which is not constitutionally authorized is, therefore, unlawful.

The importance of curial supervision and compliance with court orders is likewise deeply entrenched in Zimbabwean law. As the Supreme Court held over two decades ago:

> 'When the executive ignores the orders and judgments of the courts there is the inevitable breakdown of law and order, resulting in uncivilized chaos because the courts cannot enforce their own orders. Their jurisdiction and duty end after the delivery of judgment. The history of this case leans more towards that which is undesirable than that which is desirable in order to uphold the rule of law'.

In Rhodesia (as Zimbabwe was known prior to independence), especially under the Smith government, the rule of law was often not observed. The declaration of rights, in a series of constitutional enactments, was not justiciable. Fundamental human rights were violated with impunity. The legislature and the executive were able to deny indigenous people their political rights. A system of inequality, similar to apartheid, was in existence. Many legislative enactments were instruments of violation of human rights. Elaborate legislation, which seriously infringed rights, freedoms and liberties, was in place. The law lacked legitimacy in that it was not enacted by representatives of the population as a whole. Although judicial review existed, its reach and significance were limited. The legislature, not the law, was supreme. It was not routed in democratic values. Accordingly, the fundamental basis for a constitutional democracy and observance of the rule of law was absent.

Zimbabwe attained legitimate independence from Britain, and became a Republic in the British Commonwealth, on 18 April 1980. On the same day the Constitution (created at the Lancaster House Conference, towards the end of the previous year) came into force. It contains a justiciable Declaration of Rights. Chief among the rights protected are the right to life; the right to personal liberty; the right to freedom of conscience, expression, assembly and association; the right not to be subjected to torture or inhuman or degrading punishment or treatment; the right to be afforded a fair trial within a reasonable time by an independent and impartial court; the right to freedom from discrimination on the ground of race; and the right to protection from deprivation of property.

In the early years of independence the main area of conflict between the judiciary and the executive involved cases of detention without trial; that is, a deprivation of liberty permitted, subject to certain conditions under the law of Zimbabwe, during a declared period of public emergency. The state of emergency, which had been declared by the Smith government at its unilateral declaration of independence on 11 November 1965, and extended repeatedly every six months, was kept in force by the new government for ten years.

The first blatant failure to comply with court orders occurred in the case of the York brothers. In January 1982, two farmers, the York brothers, were arrested and charged with the illegal possession of arms of war. The state's most important witness left the country before the trial. A statement made by one of the accused to the police, apparently admitting the crime, was ruled by the trial court to be inadmissible, because it had been made as a result of police threats to arrest his family. The state case collapsed and the brothers were acquitted. The government, however, ordered their immediate detention. The High Court held that the detention was illegal as the state had failed to comply with the conditions of detention. The brothers were then re-detained on fresh detention orders, but had to be released a second time as the orders still did not comply with the necessary conditions. Again they were re-detained in terms of new orders.

It was only after this third attempt that the High Court ruled that the detention orders were validly made. The spurious reasoning advanced was that they were being held under 'investigative' detention as opposed to 'preventive' detention. Hence those rights guaranteed by the Constitution as applicable to preventive detention were not available to the detainees.

Not unexpectedly this decision was criticised as being an exercise in semantics.

On the plain facts there was no conflict between the executive and the judiciary. The Minister of Home Affairs, responsible for the police, had made a series of mistakes, and the courts were unable to uphold the detentions until those mistakes had been rectified. However, a statement made by the Minister to the court during the second detention hearing, declaring that no information would be forthcoming as to where the detainees were being held, even in the face of a court order to that effect, was indicative of just such a conflict. The same Minister, speaking in Parliament, accused the judiciary of dispensing 'injustice by handing down perverted pieces of judgment which smack of subverting the people's government'. He went on to attack the legal profession as a whole in the following paranoid terms:

> 'We are aware that certain legal practitioners are in receipt of moneys as paid hirelings, from governments hostile to our own order, in the process of seeking to destabilise us, to create a state of anarchy through the inherited legal apparatus. We promise to handle such lawyers using the appropriate technology that exists in our law and order section. This should succeed in breaking up the unholy alliance between the negative bench, the reactionary legal practitioners and governments hostile to us, some of whose representatives are in this country'.

The statement clearly represented a threat to both the independence of the judiciary and the rule of law. Members of the Law Society met the minister of justice to express their concern. The Chief Justice, after consulting the minister of justice, also issued a statement expressing concern at the attack upon the judiciary and the legal profession. The minister of justice himself put out a press release to the effect that the government recognised the role which an independent judiciary is to play in the sustenance of democratic order; and that it was government's belief that the executive and judiciary should complement each other in the fulfilment of their functions.

Although the statement of the minister of justice contained much that could be seen as recognising and supporting the independence and effectiveness of the judiciary, confusion remained as to the exact nature of the government's position on the issue. This was because a few days earlier the Prime Minister had said in parliament:

> 'The government cannot allow the technicalities of the law to fetter its hands in what is a very clear task before it, to preserve law and

order in the country. We shall, therefore, proceed as government in a manner we feel as fitting .... and some of the measurers we shall take are measures which will be extra legal'.

Taking extra-legal measure meant disobeying the law. The words clearly conveyed that it was government's policy to disobey the law whenever it considered such disobedience necessary for the preservation of law and order.

With the knowledge of hindsight, I do not believe that this criticism and disobedience of the judiciary by the executive can be dismissed as mere teething trouble – as the manifestation of a newly elected government flexing its muscles after emerging from a lengthy period of oppression under white minority rule.

A further controversial episode occurred in 1983, when six white officers of the Zimbabwe air force were charged with being involved in a serious sabotage attack on an air force base. The only evidence against them was signed confessions which they alleged were obtained as a result of torture. The trial judge found that all the accused were denied access to their legal representatives prior to making the confessions; and also that the confessions were made as a result of fear after sustained physical and mental torture. Accordingly, he held that the confessions were inadmissible, and the accused were acquitted. They were placed in preventive detention immediately upon release, but only for a short period. They were then deported from the country.

An appeal by the attorney-general to the Supreme Court which, as it happened, was comprised of three white judges, all appointed prior to 1980 (I was one of them), was dismissed. That decision was condemned by the minister of home affairs. He accused the judges of 'class bias and racism'. No contradiction of that false statement was made by any other minister, or by the attorney-general.

There is little doubt that during this early period the frequent use of detention without trial, both in instances where the courts had previously acquitted the detainees, and to circumvent the judicial process, amounted to an erosion of the rule of law. So did the government's stance in simply ignoring court orders to pay damages to victims (considered to be political enemies) of human rights violations. Since the State Liabilities Act prohibits execution, or attachment or process in the nature thereof, against state property, there is no legal remedy against such refusal. Furthermore, damage awards cannot be enforced through contempt orders. Thus, whether or not to compensate is left to the state's discretion.

In 1988 the case that brought the judiciary into conflict with the legislature was that involving the former prime minister of Rhodesia, Ian Smith. The facts were simply that, as a member of parliament, Smith had been found guilty of contempt of parliament in respect of utterances he had made in South Africa in support of apartheid policies, and in opposition to the imposition of economic sanctions against South Africa. He was suspended from service of parliament for one year and, in addition, declared disentitled to receive salary and allowances during that period. Smith applied to the High Court for an order declaring unlawful the punishment depriving him of his remuneration. At the hearing, the speaker produced a certificate which sought to stay the proceedings on the ground of parliamentary privilege. The High Court came to the conclusion that the speaker's certificate was conclusive and stayed the proceedings. On appeal, the Supreme Court had no hesitation in holding the decision to be wrong. First, it was pointed out that when a certificate from the speaker is produced, stating that the matter is one of parliamentary privilege, the court must examine the certificate in order to establish the legitimacy of the privilege claimed; and secondly, that the monetary deprivation imposed was illegal and in conflict with the Constitution. That part of the punishment (but not the suspension) was set aside.

The speaker was furious. He refused to recognise and give effect to the Supreme Court judgment. He maintained that no court of law can question a decision made by parliament. He said that he would not pay Smith unless parliament reversed its decision to suspend him without pay. He suggested that parliament might have to 'liberate itself from the Supreme Court judges; that the judiciary should not interfere with the legislature because the legislature in all Commonwealth countries is supreme'. These statements could not be allowed to go unchallenged. The Supreme Court judges, the Bar Council and the Law Society, expressed concern at the attitude of the speaker which sought to undermine the authority of the court. It was said:

> 'The judiciary is the watchdog of the country's constitution. If the legislature or the executive can disregard it at will, there is no way that the people's rights can be guaranteed. We may as well tear up that document we call our constitution'.

It was only after he had sought and obtained the authority of parliament that the speaker paid Smith. He refused to back down. So the conflict was finally resolved.

Clearly, the gravest abuse of law and order, during the first decade of the country's independence, occurred in the Matabeleland and Midlands provinces. A purported threat of 'dissident' ex-guerrilla fighters led to a counter-insurgency war, commonly known as the 'Gukurahundi' (the word refers to the first rain of summer that washes away the chaff from the previous season). In official operations by the national army's notorious North Korean trained fifth brigade, which was directly responsible to Robert Mugabe, several thousands of innocent civilians were massacred or simply disappeared. Some estimates put the number at up to 10 000 civilians. Thousands more were arbitrarily detained, brutally assaulted and often tortured. In a 1982 speech to parliament, Mugabe accurately presaged the violence in these words:

> 'An eye for an eye and an ear for an ear may not be adequate in our circumstances. We might very well demand two ears for one ear and two eyes for one eye.'

For the initial ten year of its life the Declaration of Rights in the Constitution of Zimbabwe could only amended by a unanimous vote in parliament. Not surprisingly there were no amendments to any of the rights provisions. From 11 May 1990, however, amendments to the Declaration of Rights, as well as any other provision of the Constitution, may be passed upon a vote by two-thirds of the members of parliament.

During the period 1991-2000 the parliament of Zimbabwe passed several amendments to the Declaration of Rights to the disadvantage of the individual. In early 1991 parliament passed Constitution of Zimbabwe Amendment (No.11). Two saving provisions were added to section 15 (1) (the protection against inhuman or degrading punishment or other such treatment). The first enacts that corporal punishment inflicted upon a male under the age of eighteen years shall not be held to be inhuman or degrading. This amendment effectively overruled the decision of the Supreme Court. It also runs counter to article 5 of the African Charter of Human and People's rights and to the United Nations Convention on the Rights of the Child. The second provision specifically allows sentence of death to be carried out by the method hanging. The reason for this amendment was that the Supreme Court had been due to hear a test case in which argument was to be presented on the question of whether execution by hanging was a violation of section 15 (1). Both the State and the defence had been required to adduce evidence as to the reliability of the various procedures and precautions adopted in execution by hanging; and to address the physical pain and mental anguish to which the condemned person is subjected by such method. The amendment pre-empted the court from deciding the controversial issue. The minister of justice announced to parliament that the amendment was necessary 'in order to prevent the

Supreme Court from doing away with the death sentence (a punishment sanctioned under the Constitution) via the back door'.

The eleventh amendment also altered section 16, the protection against deprivation of property without compensation. It reduced the amount payable in the event of expropriation from 'adequate compensation payable promptly' to 'fair compensation payable within a reasonable time'. It also removed the right of an expropriatee to challenge in a court of law the fairness of any compensation awarded.

In 1993 parliament passed a further amendment to section 15 (1) in order to overcome the Supreme Court judgment that an inordinate delay in carrying out a death sentence amounted to inhuman treatment.

Constitutional Amendment Act (No. 14), promulgated on 6 December 1996, amends section 22 (which had been interpreted by the Supreme Court to permit the foreign husband of a Zimbabwean citizen to reside permanently in the country, and engage in employment or other gainful activity), so as to grant neither foreign husbands nor foreign wives, of citizens, residence as of right in Zimbabwe by virtue of marriage.

On 19 April 2000, just two months before the general election was due to be held, Constitutional Amendment Act (No. 16) was passed. Whereas previously the owner of agricultural land compulsorily acquired for resettlement of people had to be compensated, the amendment spelt out that such obligation no longer pertained; it was the exclusive responsibility of the former colonial power to do so. This provision, read in context, refers to compensation with respect to the soil. It does not absolve the government from liability to compensate for improvements effected upon the land, though, unfairly, such compensation may be paid in instalments over a period of time'.

But the ultimate prohibition of access by commercial farmers to the courts came in the form of Constitutional Amendment Act (No.17), promulgated on 14 September 2005. It effectively vests the ownership of agricultural land, compulsorily acquired for resettlement purposes in conformity with the land reform programme, in the state; and ousts the jurisdiction of the courts to entertain any challenge concerning such acquisition.

Constitutional Amendments 16 &17 have been roundly, and aptly, condemned as being:

> '...without modern parallel in any constitutional democracy worthy of its name. They set Zimbabwe apart from all member states of SADC, the British Commonwealth and the African Union, which

> function as constitutional democracies. They violate Zimbabwe's international law obligations, most immediately through its membership of the African Union. They entail the abrogation of constitutionalism and elevate the fiat of the executive and legislature over the entrenched core provisions of the Constitution. They certify the existence of a totalitarian state.'

The essence of a constitution is that it should, among other things, lay down the rules of conduct for state organs. Parliament, which is established and exists in terms of the constitution, should be subordinate to it. It should not be able to change the constitution and diminish or dilute the scope of a fundamental right or protection, whenever it considers it politically expedient to do so.

Yet another manner in which the rule of law has been undermined, is by the unreasonable utilisation of the Presidential Pardon. In terms of section 31I of the Constitution, the President has a right to grant a pardon, amnesty or clemency, to convicted prisoners. There are no set criteria upon which this power is exercised, and in the absence of such, abuse has been inevitable. What has been happening over the years is that the President has been using this pardon to free those of his political party, or members of the Central Intelligence Organisation (CIO), convicted of politically motivated crimes.

An instance of the flagrant abuse of the Presidential Pardon is the Kombayi case. Patrick Kombayi, a flamboyant businessman, contested as an opposition political candidate for the City of Gweru constituency in the 1990 general election. During the run up to the election, there were indications that his opponent, the ruling party's candidate and Vice President, could be embarrassed. As a result there was much violence and tension in Gweru, the culmination of which was the almost fatal shooting of Kombayi, by a member of the CIO and a party loyalist. These two men were ultimately convicted and sentenced to long terms of imprisonment by a magistrate's court. Their appeal to the Supreme Court was dismissed. Within a day of that order, the President published a proclamation pardoning the two criminals.

More unforgivably, Clemency Order of 1998 pardoned all human rights violations and atrocities perpetrated by all parties during the so-called Gukurahundi war.

A gross breach of the rule of law, absent any hint of legitimacy, occurred in January 1999, with the arrest, detention, interrogation and torture, by the army's military police of two journalists over an article they published in a daily newspaper about an alleged coup plot by a few officers. The journalists were held for over a week before being placed in the custody of the police. Neither the President, nor any minister, nor the commissioner of police, openly complained that the action of the military authority was in violation of the law. There was no expression that the power to arrest and detain civilians vested solely in the police working with the courts. The perception was, therefore, that the military authority may operate beyond the reach of the law; this more especially when the President announced publicly that the journalists had forfeited their right to legal protection by having acted in such a grossly dishonest manner. The reason for non-intervention professed by the commissioner of police was 'because the nature of the enquiry involved highly sensitive matters of national security which could not be dealt with by my officers'. To complete the scenario: The journalists laid criminal charges against the perpetrators of their illegal detentions and torture. Both the attorney-general and the commissioner of police exhibited not the slightest interest in investigating the complaints. In the event, the journalists sought, and were granted, an order from the Supreme Court directing the commissioner of police to institute a comprehensive and diligent investigation of the offences alleged to have been committed with a view to the prosecution of all persons against whom there was a reasonable suspicion of complicity. Regretfully, nothing was done to bring the offenders to justice. The commissioner of police simply refused to perform a duty imposed upon the police force by the law of the land.

Undoubtedly the pivotal event of the year 2000 was the rejection of the government sponsored draft constitution, in mid February, by 54 % of the voters in a referendum. It sparked off a series of extreme responses from government that all but destroyed the rule of law, and has had ruinous international and economic consequences for the country.

A few days after the referendum results were announced, there were large-scale, synchronized invasions of white owned agricultural land, 86% of which had changed hands since independence, and only after government had declined to exercise options to purchase.

The initial invasions were followed by a massive and rapid expansion of the process, which required considerable pre-planning and logistical support. There was substantial government involvement in carrying out the invasions. Prospective occupiers were transported in an assortment of government vehicles to the farms which had been targeted. Once in place, the occupiers received monthly payments and regular food supplies which were delivered in government vehicles.

Only a small number of the invaders were actually war veterans; most were too young to have taken part in the liberation struggle. Many probably participated in the exercise primarily because they were unemployed and had been offered payment; although some did so because they wished to obtain land. There is little doubt that government orchestrated the initial farm invasions, and once underway, condoned and supported them.

The unlawful countrywide occupation of white owned productive agricultural land resulted in an application being brought before the High Court by the Commercial Farmers Union. The order sought was against the chairman of the War Veterans Association and the commissioner of police. It was granted by consent on 17 March 2000. It declared that the occupation of farms by persons claiming a right to do so, in pursuit of an entitlement to demonstrate against the iniquity of land distribution, was unlawful. All such persons were ordered to vacate within twenty-four hours. The commissioner of police was directed to instruct his officers and members to enforce the law.

Despite having agreed to the order, the commissioner of police applied within a few days to amend it on the ground that he did not have the manpower to effect the removal of those in unlawful occupation; and that, in any event, their right of occupation merited a political and not a legal solution; and as such, was not promotive of the rule of law. The amendment was refused. The order stood. It was not, however, obeyed. The President criticised it as nonsensical. This it clearly was not. To have ruled any other way would have amounted to a violation of the law. The unlawful occupations, with the encouragement of government, proceeded at an accelerated pace.

Then there was another order by consent, this time granted by the Supreme Court. The order again declared that the entry of uninvited persons on commercial farming properties was unlawful. It required the respondents, who were the ministers most closely concerned with agricultural land reform, the commissioner of police, and those under their control, not to give sanction to the entry, or continued occupation, of farms, by persons involved in resettlement, until all legal requirements and procedures had been fulfilled. The order was not meant to prevent the government from pursuing land resettlement. Certainly, that was neither the objective nor the policy of the courts. The effect of the order was that land resettlement should be carried out within the framework of the Constitution, and in compliance with the provisions of the Land Acquisition Act; and not by unlawful invasion.

Finally, in this regrettable saga, the Supreme Court once more declared that the relevant ministers and the commissioner of police should comply immediately with the prior orders. It was said:

> 'Wicked things have been done, and continue to be done. They must be stopped. Common law crimes have been, and are being, committed with impunity. Laws made by parliament have been flouted by the government. The activities of the past months must be condemned'.

In elucidation it was pointed out that:

> 'The settling of people on farms has been entirely haphazard and unlawful. A network of organisations, operating with complete disregard for the law, has been allowed to take over from government. War veterans, villagers and unemployed townspeople, have simply moved on to farms. They have been supported, encouraged, transported and financed, by party official, public servants, the CIO and the army. The rule of law has been overthrown in the commercial farming areas and farmers and farm workers on occupied farms have been denied the protection of the law'.

The order made was, likewise, ignored. The official stance taken up was that land distribution is a political and not a legal matter, which cannot be resolved by the application of 'the little law of trespass'. The courts were to keep out of the arena. The President said that he would not allow the police to move against the farm invaders, who are merely taking over land which was 'stolen' from blacks by whites.

It is completely unacceptable to qualify the rule of law in this way. Rulers who pick and choose which laws they wish to obey by defining certain matters as 'political', because it suites them, thereby vitiate the principle of equality before the law, setting one standard for themselves and another for the people they govern. That is at variance with elementary justice as well as international norms.

In October 2000 the President issued Clemency Order No.1. It granted an amnesty to those who kidnapped, tortured and assaulted people and burnt people's houses and other possessions, as a way of politically intimidating them during the period from 1 January to 31 July 2000; (that is, in connection with 12 and 13 February Constitutional Referendum, and 24 and 25 June elections). The amnesty meant that those arrested and facing trial for such serious offences were released, and no new investigations and prosecutions may take place into their crimes.

In the main, these crimes were committed by loyalists of the ruling party against supporters, actual or perceived, of opposition political parties. The effect of the amnesty created the belief that political violence will be condoned and those responsible for it are above the law, and will go unpunished. This is extremely dangerous. It sends the wrong signal, suggesting that election related violence will be tolerated – a bad precedent for future elections. There are reports of persons who have benefited from the amnesty taking violent action against those who reported them to the police. In the words of Amnesty International:

> 'This pardon represents a lost chance for justice and the possibility of breaking the cycle of impunity that has riddled Zimbabwe. By failing to tackle impunity for gross human rights abuses, the order provides no deterrent either to continuing human rights abuses or contempt for international human rights law'.

Other disturbing conduct at about this time was the harassment of the High Court and Supreme Court judges by war veterans and followers. They called upon judges to resign or face removal by force. The minister of information spearheaded this campaign by accusing the Supreme Court of being biased in favour of white landowners at the expense of the landless majority. He called on me to resign.

Such attacks show total disrespect for the rule of law and the process of the Constitution which guarantees judicial independence. Judges should not be made to feel apprehensive of their personal safety. They should not be subjected to government intimidation in the hope that they would become more compliant, and rule in favour of the executive. They should not face anything other than legitimate criticism arising from what was done in the discharge of judicial duty.

The invasion of the Supreme Court building on the morning of 24 November 2000, by close to two hundred war veterans and followers, was nothing but disgraceful. In the course of entry the policeman on guard was assaulted. The mob rushed from the main entrance through the building to the courtroom, where the judges were about to hear a constitutional application brought by the Commercial Farmers Union. They shouted political slogans and even called for the judges to be killed. They stood on chairs, benches and tables, in a gesture of absolute contempt for the institution of the courts as the third essential organ of a democratic government. Such deplorable behaviour sent the clearest message that the rule of law was not to be adhered to. The invasion lasted an hour. It disrupted, as it was intended to do, the proceedings of the court. There is good reason to believe that it had been instigated and organised by the minister of information.

Disappointingly, yet expectedly, there was no official condemnation of the incident. Not a word was heard from the President, the minister of justice, or the attorney- general. Only the president of the law society spoke out boldly against it, as he had done on previous occasions when the judiciary and been the subject of threats or unfounded criticism. To him, and the legal profession he represents, go much appreciation for the support shown to the judiciary.

On 14 December 2000, President Mugabe, speaking at his party's congress, disowned the courts. With reference to the land issue he said:

> 'The courts can do what they want. They are not courts for our people and we shall not even be defending ourselves in these courts.'

One year later the present Chief Justice, with the concurrence of three newly appointed judges, predictably set aside the Supreme Court's earlier judgment, and endorsed the government land acquisition policy. There was one dissention. The majority found that the government had taken sufficient steps to restore the rule of law on commercial farms. It had achieved this by passing the Rural Land Occupiers (Protection from Eviction) Act, which legalised the unlawful occupations of land that had taken place; and the facts established that the police were adopting adequate measures to prevent crime in the commercial farming areas. The ratio for this volte face is highly questionable. Non-the-less, the majority decision provided the legal legitimacy from the highest court that the government had been seeking for its 'land' programme. It allowed the government to claim that the entire programme is lawful, constitutional and in accordance with the rule of law. This is blatantly not so.

The fast-track land reform programme remains much in force today. In theory it was meant to correct "historical imbalances", and to hand land to landless black Zimbabweans, through a one-man one farm policy. Pursued in a most chaotic, ruthless, uncontrolled and violent manner, it has resulted in about 4500 white commercial farmers being forced off their land, and 350 000 farm labourers being deprived of their livelihood. The grave atrocities committed against white farmers are legend. In 2000 alone seven suffered violent deaths at the hands of the invaders (the deaths now total 16). Many others have been subjected to acts of attempted murder, grievous assaults, torture and abduction; their homesteads looted and often set on fire, valuable farm equipment and crops stolen or destroyed, and productive land senselessly ravaged. Farm labourers have been intimidated, threatened and beaten mercilessly. The victims have been denied the protection of the police; the pretext being that the occupation of land is a political and not a legal issue. Any intervention provided is solely to enable the invaders assume control of land. The reality is that in commercial farming areas throughout the country, the rule of law has become a myth.

There has been little improvement in the country's steep economic decline, wide spread food shortages, high unemployment and politically motivated violence, since the formation of the unity government on 11 February of this year. And this, notwithstanding, that the Global Political Agreement, reached on 15 September 2008, committed the opposing political parties to a cessation of violence, the conduct of a comprehensive, transparent and nonpartisan land audit (which was not to reverse the land reform programme, but to do away with multiple farm ownership), and to ensuring security of tenure for all landholders, with land to be given irrespective of race.

Yet, in a document, dated as recently as 27 August 2009, the ministry of lands and resettlement effectively withdrew from the undertaking to compile a land audit, citing an expense problem. It now recommends that:

(a) land acquisition and redistribution should continue given the incremental demand for land;

(b) no foreigner should be allowed to own rural agricultural land;

(c) agricultural land should be excluded from the protection afforded by Bilateral Investment Promotion and Protection agreements;

(d) prosecutions of farmers resisting to move off acquired land should continue.

In this year alone more than 80 commercial farms have been forcibly seized, in accord with the stated objective of the ZANU-PF party that every white farmer is to be removed from agricultural land. Over 6600 farm workers have been made homeless by new occupiers, who are not engaged in productive farming. Violence is rife, with little done to eradicate it. The number of white commercial farmers has shrunk to about 250. They are occupying land greatly reduced in size, and under constant and violent pressure of eviction. At a conference held in Pretoria at the end of September, the president of the Commercial Farmers Union, said:

> 'The situation is that we're receiving an even bigger hiding than before. Although everything seems to be fine on the outside, the rule of law just is not there. It's applied very selectively.'

Despite enduring constant threats, intimidation, harassment, assaults and arrests, many commercial farmers have fearlessly continued to engage the government in legal proceedings in an endeavour either to retain, or regain, occupation of agricultural land, or their valuable personal possessions.

On 11 October 2007, and only after the courts in Zimbabwe had refused them relief, Mike Campbell (Private) Limited and William Michael Campbell, filed an application before the Southern African Development Community (SADC) Tribunal, contesting the acquisition by the Republic of Zimbabwe of agricultural land, pursuant to the country's 'fast-track' land reform exercise. The challenge was based on the ground that the land reform policy, and compulsory acquisitions in terms thereof, breached the SADC Treaty, signed by President Mugabe on 17 August 1992, ratified by parliament on 17 November 1992, and operational as from 30 September 1993. The Tribunal comprised the former Chief Justice of Mauritius, as President, and four other eminent judges of the region.

The challenge gave rise to several interlocutory applications. The first concerned a successful claim for interim relief pending the final disposal of the matter. The second involved the interventions of 77 additional individuals who faced similar interferences with agricultural land. That application was granted and interim relief extended also to those interveners.

In its judgment of 28 November 2008, the Tribunal found that it had jurisdiction to entertain the application. It further held, unanimously, that the applicants had been denied access to the courts of Zimbabwe, and that fair compensation was payable for the expropriation of the land. It was said:

> 'It is difficult for us to understand the rationale behind excluding compensation for such land, given the clear legal position in international law. It is the right of the applicants under international law to be paid, and the correlative duty of the respondent to pay, fair compensation. Moreover, the respondent cannot rely on its national law, or its constitution, to avoid an international law obligation to pay compensation'.

By a majority of four to one, the Tribunal ruled that the applicants had been discriminated against on the ground of race. It unanimously directed that the government take:

> 'all necessary measures, through its agents, to protect the possession, occupation and ownership of the land of the applicants .... and to take all appropriate measures to ensure that no action is taken, pursuant to Amendment 17, directly or indirectly, whether by its agents or by others, to evict from, or interfere with, the peaceful residence on, and of those farms by, the applicants.'

And that those applicants, whose property had already been expropriated, were to be paid fair compensation by the government, on or before 30 June 2009.

Despite the fact that in terms of article 32 (3) of the Treaty the judgment is final and binding, the government refuses to comply with it.

On 18 December 2008, the deputy attorney-general stated in writing that:

> 'the policy decision taken by the government to the judgment is that all prosecutions of defaulting farmers ...... should now be resumed'.

The minister responsible for land reform and resettlement said that the Tribunal was 'day dreaming', and that the government was 'not going to reverse the land reform exercise'.

A speech delivered by the Deputy Chief Justice on 12 January 2009, at the opening of the legal year, sought to impugn the judgment on the basis that the Tribunal lacked jurisdiction to hear and determine the case. The following month, in the course of his birthday celebrations, the President denigrated the Tribunal's decision as 'nonsense' and 'of no consequence'. Prosecutors and magistrates were coached by the ministry of justice and the attorney-general's office, at various workshops around the country, on how to react to the judgment, which was disparaged as 'not binding'. Eviction orders issued against white farmers were to be complied with, as in the past.

In the wake of the continued seizure of more land from the remaining few white farmers, and numerous serious and persistent threats to their very lives, some of the beneficiaries of the judgment again turned to the Tribunal for legal protection. (The Campbell family were badly assaulted after the Tribunal had granted an interim protection order in their favour, before the final hearing, in the course of which assaults they were given papers to sign seeking the abandonment of their case before the Tribunal).

On 5 June 2009, the Tribunal, recognising the urgency of the matter, issued an ex tempore order directing the government's failure to comply with the judgment, to the SADC Summit for its attention, and granted an order for costs in favour of the applicants.

Prior to the holding of the SADC Summit in early September 2009, at Kinshasa, the government decided to pull out of the SADC Tribunal after the minister of justice declared it 'unlawful'. In a letter delivered to the Tribunal on 10 August 2009, the minister wrote:

> 'The purported application of the provisions of the Protocol on Zimbabwe is a serious violation of international law. There was never any basis upon which the Tribunal could seek or purport to found jurisdiction on Zimbabwe based on the Protocol which has not yet been ratified by two-thirds of the total membership of SADC. As we are unaware of any other basis upon which the Tribunal can exercise jurisdiction over Zimbabwe, we hereby advise that, henceforth, we will not appear before the Tribunal and neither will we respond to any action or suit instituted or be pending against the Republic of Zimbabwe before the Tribunal. For the same reasons, any decisions that the Tribunal may have or may make in future against the Republic of Zimbabwe, are null and void'.

The validity of the minister's opinion has been contested by senior counsel who appeared before the Tribunal on behalf of the applicants, on the following grounds:

(a) Zimbabwe is a signatory to the SADC Treaty.

(b) Zimbabwe is bound to the Protocol despite not ratifying it. c) Zimbabwe has conceded the SADC Tribunal's jurisdiction.

(c) The SADC Tribunal has held that Zimbabwe is subject to its jurisdiction. It is the designated SADC organ conferred by the Treaty with the authority to interpret the provisions of the Treaty; hence it is the body to decide whether a State is bound by the Treaty and the Protocol, and subject to its jurisdiction.

This view of the controversy is shared unequivocally by the organisation known as Zimbabwe Lawyers for Human Rights. It points out that articles 35 and 38 of the Tribunal Protocol, upon which the minister relied for the averment that the Tribunal was not properly constituted because it was not ratified by two-thirds of SADC members, were both repealed by article

16(2) of the Treaty. The effect was to make the Tribunal an integral part of both the Treaty and the Institution of SADC. The repeal specifically excluded the Tribunal Protocol from the usual requirement for ratification before it could come into force and effect.

On 15 and 16 September 2009, representatives of the premier bar associations and rule of law institutions on the African continent, met in Arusha, and issued a communiqué on the status of the Tribunal. It expressed disapproval of the reasons offered by the minister of justice justifying his contention that the Tribunal lacked legitimacy; and supported the grounds advanced for the opposing view. Furthermore, it observed:

> 'The failure of the Government of Zimbabwe to comply with a court decision, whether of a domestic or international tribunal is consistent with its endemic culture of defiance of court orders that it dislikes.
>
> In Zimbabwe the Government dismantled the Supreme Court and the High Court when they were seen as issuing decisions which the Government disliked through forcing out judges and hiring "politically correct" individuals. Its current thrust to destroy the SADC judicial organ is consistent with the Government's conduct in dealing with judicial organs it dislikes'.

The application of Gramara (Private) Limited v Government of Zimbabwe is due to be argued in the High Court on 24 November 2009. The relief sought is a declaration that the ruling of the SADC Tribunal in the Campbell matter be registered with the High Court for the purpose of its enforcement in Zimbabwe. The crucial point the presiding judge will have to decide is whether the Tribunal lawfully exercised jurisdiction over Zimbabwe based on the Tribunal Protocol. Whatever determination is made, the overwhelming probability is an appeal to the Supreme Court by the losing party. (The Deputy Chief Justice has already revealed his hand, as has the High Court judge, whose nomination as a member of the SADC Tribunal has now been withdrawn). Inevitably there will be an inordinate delay before the issue is finally resolved. And the longer it remains alive domestically, the more advantage is to be gained by government. For in the situation obtaining, it is unlikely that SADC will entertain the Tribunal's request to consider enforcement steps of its judgment against Zimbabwe as a SADC member.

A more definitive success was achieved by thirteen Dutch nationals, whose large commercial farms in Zimbabwe had been expropriated, despite the existence of a Bilateral Investment Treaty concluded by Zimbabwe and the Netherlands. On 22

April 2009, they received a total award of Euros 8 220 000 as compensatory damages from an arbitral panel, appointed by the International Centre for Settlement of Investment Disputes, Washington, D.C. No appeal is pending, but payment is still to be made.

The persistent onslaught suffered by the rule of law and democracy in Zimbabwe cannot be underestimated. Legality and constitutionality have been cast aside. Forces of violence, intimidation and disorder have been unleashed, and allowed to prevail particularly, but certainly not exclusively, in the implementation of the fast- track land reform programme. A programme that has all to do with power politics; and nothing to do with the professed continuation of the liberation struggle to bring about economic emancipation for the landless majority. The timing of its introduction, after a delay of two decades since independence, proves the point. The law enforcement agencies have either actively collaborated in these lawless activities, or simply declined to afford protection, sanctuary and good order, in the fulfilment of their fundamental duties.

There is urgent need to witness real progress on the part of the inclusive government on critical issues like restoring the rule of law, adhering to international treaty obligations, respecting human rights and guaranteeing freedom of speech, and freedom of assembly and association. Law enforcement agencies will have to be overhauled so that they again become professional, politically neutral forces that respect the human rights of all Zimbabweans, and enforce the law on a fair and impartial basis. Sham politically motivated prosecutions must cease. So must the unlawful detentions, arrests, torture and harassment, of human rights defenders and independent journalists. New private media should be licensed and international journalists allowed to practice openly.

That said, it would be remiss of me were I not to acknowledge and acclaim, the on- going courageous struggle against oppression and injustice, by local organisations such as, Zimbabwe Lawyers for Human Rights, Crisis in Zimbabwe Coalition, Justice for Agriculture, Zimbabwe Peace Project, as well as by many prominent human rights lawyers; often to the detriment of their personal safety. Names that immediately come to mind (and there are many others) are Beatrice Mtetwa, Arnold Tsunga, Alec Muchadehama, Justina Mukoko and Jenny Williams, three of whom have received international awards.

In the last few months, the Supreme Court granted an order permanently staying the prosecution of Justina Mukoko on charges relating to terrorism.

She had been abducted from the family home at daybreak, while in her nightgown and bare foot, and not seen for three weeks. She later testified that she was held at secret locations while being severely tortured by state security agents, in an attempt to extract a false confession.

More recently, a High Court judge, ordered the government to restore to the British company, African Consolidated Resources Limited, the right of title to claims in the Marange diamond fields, which had been seized in October 2006, and allocated to the state owned Zimbabwe Mining Development Corporation; and the return of 129,400 carats of diamonds confiscated by the police in January 2007. The learned judge ended by saying:

> 'The papers before me paint a gloomy picture of the duty to protect our national heritage by those constitutionally charged with that responsibility'.

Regrettably, the police and the army continue to deny African Consolidated Resources access to the diamond fields (a site of grave military atrocities), and the Mining Corporation has not halted its drilling operations. Both activities are in breach of the judge's order that the noting of an appeal would not suspend the operation of the judgment.

Time will tell whether these two judgments signify the beginning of a genuine shift in judicial approach. But, at the very least, they should be taken as a pointer that Zimbabwean courts will not rule invariably in favour of the state.

The formation of the power-sharing government was welcomed by most right- thinking Zimbabweans. It has resulted in an end to rampant inflation and in a fair measure of economic stability. Though now threatened by policy differences, the slow pace of reforms, and feuding over top executive positions it, nevertheless, represents a glimmer of hope of a return to democracy, and with it international recognition and financial aid. So, it is critical that it holds together. For fragile as it is, it is a substantial improvement from the history of the past, and is stumbling forward on a road to recovery, although one beset by numerous potholes.

Zimbabwe's natural and human resources were once the envy of Africa; and they still could be. But no one will invest in the county until they are confident in the legal environment. It is simply basic economics. Capital is a coward, as the saying goes. Foreign investors, not to mention Zimbabwe businessmen, want to be assured that the rule of law will be observed and adhered to, and that their investments will be safe, before they put money into the economy. What this requires is positive political will to heal past wounds. It requires political leaders who place the interest of the people of Zimbabwe ahead of their own. Most of all it requires that all Zimbabweans stand up for their rights; and take responsibility for, and play a role in, the democratic changes and fundamental liberties they want to be able to enjoy. Meanwhile, as the Portuguese say, 'a luta continua': the struggle goes on...

Justice in a Secularising and Pluralising Society

THE MOST REVEREND & RT. HON. DR. JOHN SENTAMU

Archbishop of York

7 December 2010

INTRODUCTION

I am very grateful to the Bar Council for the invitation to deliver this Fourth Annual International Rule of Law Lecture. The previous International Rule of Law Lectures began with the successful inaugural lecture given, in 2007, by Judge Philippe Kirsh, President of the International Criminal Court, who dealt with **the challenges facing his Court and of making international criminal justice a respected reality**.

The second International Rule of Law Lecture was given by Judge Johann Kriegler, former judge of the Constitutional Court of South Africa on *'The rule of law in post-colonial Africa: a British legacy?'*

The third lecture, delivered, in 2009, by the former Chief Justice of the Supreme Court of Zimbabwe, Judge Anthony Gubbay, focused on *'The progressive erosion of the Rule of Law in Independent Zimbabwe'*.

And tonight I will endeavour to explore with you the question of *'Justice in a Secularising and Pluralising Society'*

It is almost inevitable that speaking to such an esteemed gathering I would have to begin with a true-ism about lawyers.

As a former lawyer and an Advocate of the High Court of Uganda myself, and a Honorary Master Bencher of Gray's Inn, the similarity between a Lawyer and a rhinoceros is obvious for all to experience: **thick-skinned**, **short-sighted** and **ready to charge**. I am also reminded of my mother's dictum: do not point a finger at anyone; because when you do there are at least three others pointing back at you.

With that caveat in place I think it is safe to tell the story of a dispute that once arose between the Archangel Gabriel and the Devil over the borders between Heaven and Hell. Satan was summoned into heaven and was told that the Court of Heaven was unhappy that the fence he had erected between heaven and hell seemed to have moved and that the Devil was encroaching on territory that was not his. Satan started to dissemble and argue, giving various excuses and flimsy explanations until the Archangel Gabriel finally said: "I'm afraid none of that is acceptable. You either move the fence back or I'll sue." At this point the devil collapsed into a heap of mirth and started laughing uncontrollably. "And where exactly," asked the Devil "do you think heaven is going to find a lawyer?"

LAW & MORALS

I am aware that tonight this lecture is attended by a wide range of people, not all of whom are lawyers or soon-to-be lawyers. However, I would like to begin with a question to you all - seeking your legal opinion.

Many of you are aware of the reports of the pension that was paid to the former Chief Executive of the Royal Bank of Scotland, Sir Fred Goodwin. In 2008 the bank reported its end of year results. Their loss of £24 billion was the biggest in British history and some twenty thousand jobs were under threat.

As a result of his taking early retirement in October 2008 (as part of the bank's agreement to be bailed out by the Government) Sir Fred was claiming his due annual pension of almost seven hundred thousand pounds per year as provided for under his contract.

Now judging solely on the facts before us that Sir Fred was contractually entitled to claim this pension, can I ask you gathered here, in your legal opinion, how many of you think - from a legal point of view – that it was lawful for Sir Fred to receive his pension? Please raise your hands.

Thank you.

Now a second question. How many of you believe it is right and just on a *moral* basis – not a legal basis this time, but a *moral* basis - for Sir Fred to receive his pension? Please raise your hands.

This increasing division in our society between what is legal on the one hand and what is moral on the other is one of the challenges faced not only by law makers but by our wider society, and it is this that will be the basis of my lecture tonight. However, before leaving the issue of banking, I think it is worth making two further comments.

The first is that I think we should be very careful about deciding the question of Sir Fred's pension in the alternative jurisdiction proposed, in

2009, by the Deputy Leader of the Labour Party, that of ***"the court of public opinion"***.[1] Whilst I acknowledge that this court sits every hour of every day in the media, and delivers its verdicts in the views of reporters, columnists and newspaper editorials, and by Radio and Television, blogs and tweets, we need to say No to trying our cases - whatever their apparent rights or wrongs – in this manner.

The court of public opinion is a Kangaroo Court, which has no place in British Jurisprudence except at the ballot box.

It is a long established principle of English Law, dating back to the sixteenth century, that the accused is innocent until proven guilty. This vital principle of innocence has its roots in ancient times.

In 359 AD a trial took place where a local governor, Numerius of Narbonne, was accused of raiding his own coffers. There was little proof but that didn't stop the whispers and accusations. Still, the prosecutor was convinced the governor was guilty and said as much to the judge, the Roman Emperor Julian.

At his trial the governor denied the charges and the case was due to be dismissed. The prosecutor was furious: "Oh, illustrious Caesar", he raged, "if it is sufficient to deny, what hereafter will become of the guilty?"

Emperor Julian's response has been repeated in countless trials for the past 1600 years: "If it suffices to accuse, what then will become of the innocent?"

It is not the first time the idea of the presumption of innocence appears in history, but it is a good summary of the principle: accusations of guilt are not enough unless you can prove them.

I do not know enough about the facts of Sir Fred's employment to know whether he is contractually entitled to receive all or part of his pension – certainly if he has worked the hours and earned his pension rights, the matter is not as straightforward as some would have us believe - but it is clear to me that the one place *not* to try this particular matter is in '*the court of public opinion*' where the judge, jury and executioner always stands ready to shout "off with their head".

My second point on the banking issue brings me back to my theme for tonight and comes from the erstwhile Chairman of HSBC, Stephen Green,

1 Interview with Harriet Harman on Andrew Marr Show, 1 March 2009***

an ordained priest in the Church of England, and author of the book *Good Value, Reflections on Money, Morality and an uncertain world.'* [2]

In his submission to the Parliamentary Commission on Banking Standards, Mr Green argued that swathes of the banking sector simply lost their moral compass in the *"go-go years"*, causing a "major breakdown in trust". He continued:

"It is as if, too often, people had given up asking whether something was the right thing to do, and focused only whether it was legal and complied with the rules… We should remember that no amount of rules and regulation will be sufficient if the culture does not encourage people to do the right thing."[3]

I believe there is a pressing need for our culture, and not only the banking sector, but our wider culture to rediscover a way that both encourages and enables people to do the right thing. Stephen Green's comments point us back to the third and final unanswered question regarding Sir Fred's pension. Not simply is it legal or is it moral but perhaps most importantly is it right? Is it the right thing? Posed accurately, the question for me is whether it is just.

And it is answering that question that we must bring into the equation not only law and morals but also religion.

Why? Because given the **potency** of **Money**, **Party Politics** and **Organised Religion**, how can we deliver **justice** in a Secularising and Pluralising Society?

LAW, RELIGION AND MORALS

In case anyone is sitting there thinking, well of course Archbish, you would say that wouldn't you? Let me say that I am supported in this view by perhaps one of the greatest jurists this country has ever produced. But don't take my word for it.

Just visit the Facebook page entitled, "The Lord Denning Appreciation Society", where the fan club currently stands at over twelve thousand people! Two of the comments on the page appealed to me. The first from

[2] "Good Value: Reflections on Money, Morality and an uncertain world' by Stephen Green (Pub Allen Lane; July 2009)

[3] Lord Green's submission to the Future of Banking Commission:on 15 March 2010 Paras 77 and 84: http://www.publications.parliament.uk/pa/jt201314/jtselect/jtpcbs/27/27v_we54.htm.

Mr. Peter Jones, who said: "When Superman wants his children to behave, he tells them about Lord Denning." Another comment - from Rose Latham - said simply, "One word sums up this man: Legend."

Lord Denning was unquestionably the greatest and most influential English judge of the second half of the 20th century. He was known simply as "the people's judge". Lord Woolf said of him: "Until Denning's time, on the whole it was the great criminal cases that caught the public imagination. With him, for the first time, it was the civil cases, because he was projecting the little man against the big battalions."

Justice in a Secularising and Pluralising Society can best be delivered if Law, Religion and Morals are inter-mingled. My position derives from Denning's famous comment: "Without religion, no morality; without morality, no law."

Lord Denning expounded upon this basic precept in his 1953 book, *The Changing Law,* where he wrote:

> "The severance of these ideas—of law from morality, and of religion from law — belongs very distinctly to the later stages of the evolution of modern thought.
>
> This severance has gone a great way. Many people now think that religion and law have nothing in common. The law, they say, governs our dealings with our fellows, whereas religion concerns our dealings with God. Likewise, they hold that law has nothing to do with morality. Law lays down rigid rules which must be obeyed without questioning whether they are right or wrong. Its function is to keep order, not to do justice.
>
> The severance has, I think, gone much too far. Although religion, law and morals can be separated, they are nevertheless still very much dependent on one another. Without religion, there can be no morality, there can be no law." [4]

In my lecture this evening I hope to explore further Denning's view and to explain why, in my opinion, this separation of Law, Religion and Morals has gone too far.

Justice in a Secularising and Pluralising Society would become much harder to deliver if this separation were to continue. Hermetically sealed spheres of understanding of Law, of Religion, of Morals, would not create

[4] *The Changing Law* by Lord Denning, London : Stevens, 1953.

a society where the Rule of Law is paramount. Competing rights of Law, of Religion and of Morals would trump each other. Turf warfare could lead to the 'law of the jungle'. Situational morality, for example, led to water-boarding for Guantanamo Bay detainees, and trumped both the Rule of Law and Religion.

I was surprised to read Janet Daly's comment in *The Sunday Telegraph* of 13 November 2010, page 26, that

> 'We can't afford moral certainty about torture… who has the right to decide that lives should be sacrificed for an unwavering moral dictum?'[5]

LAW & RELIGION

As a young law student I greatly admired Lord Denning. And when I started practising, both at the Bar and the Bench, his judgments, and those of Lord Atkins[6] were a real guide to me – surprise, surprise. They have also inspired my thinking for this lecture.

The influence of religion on law in this country, to Lord Denning, was obvious, but it is not so obvious in today's United Kingdom. In the four nations, which make up Britain, religion, morals and law have been indistinguishably mixed together – influenced largely by the Ten Commandments. For example, you find the *first* Commandment which is religious:

> "God spoke all these words: I am the Lord your God; you shall have no other gods before me."

You find the *fifth* Commandment which is a moral precept.

> "Honour your father and thy mother; that your days may be long in the land which the Lord thy God is giving you."

You find the *eighth* Commandment which is a legal duty:

> "You shall not steal."

5 http://www.telegraph.co.uk/comment/columnists/janetdaley

6 See the celebrated case of Donoghue v Stevenson - *[1932] AC 562, 580 (HL). Donoghue v Stevenson* - where Lord Atkins argued the law of Negligence on the basis of the question, 'Who is my neighbour?' (from the parable in Luke Chapter 10).

This intermingling has served the United Kingdom very well. But the severance of three ideas – of law from morality, and of religion from law – has, very wrongly in my view, led many people, and law-makers in particular, to think that religion and law have nothing in common.

The function of Law is to keep order, not to do justice.

Many of the fundamental principles of the laws of the United Kingdom have been derived from the Judaeo-Christian religion. Sadly, these principles are challenged by a changing and a changed United Kingdom which treats religion as something private, for woolly minds. A Secularising and a Pluralising Society could easily become a society which is moral but with no compass.

I know that it is our duty to be just and fair in all our dealings. But our concept of justice has been moulded by the Judaeo-Christian teaching of love.

Archbishop William Temple, one of my predecessors, said that,

> "It is axiomatic that love should be the predominant Christian impulse and that the primary form of love in social organisation is Justice."

This is summed up in Luke's Gospel, Chapter 10, when a lawyer asked Jesus of Nazareth, *"Teacher, what must I do to inherit eternal life?"*

'He said to him, "What is written in the law? What do you read there?" He answered, "You shall love the Lord your God with all your heart, and with all your soul, and with all your strength, and with all your mind; and your neighbour as yourself." And he said to him, "You have given the right answer; do this, and you will live".[7]

This precept – love towards God and love towards neighbour – is a precept of religion. Nevertheless in many affairs of life, love can only find expression through justice, which is God-like.

Religion, law and morality need to be brought together under the great tent of love.

This is the great lesson of the interview between Jesus of Nazareth and the Lawyer recorded in the tenth chapter of the Gospel of Luke. The story of the traveller who fell among robbers and was helped, not by a Priest or the Levite, but by a Samaritan.

[7] Luke 10:25b-28

Love of God: Love of neighbour: "Go and do likewise, and you shall live", so said Jesus of Nazareth. See yourself as under God and under the rule of law; and love your neighbour as yourself. For this contains the law and the commandment.

Law, religion and morals inhabiting the same tent of humanity.

It is a truism to say that what we think and what we do depends largely on what we believe, and what we value most, rather than on what powers and laws we invoke or are invoked against us.

The question for me isn't whether these values suit us, but whether we suit them. A sane person doesn't say, "The law of gravity doesn't suit me, so I can ignore it and walk over the edge of Beachy Head in security". We reject these values at our peril.

Lord Denning was right when he said that, if we seek truth and justice, we can't find it by argument and debate, nor by reading and thinking, but only (as the Book of Common Prayer says) by 'the maintenance of true religion and justice/virtue'.

Religion concerns the spirit in humanity, whereby we are able to recognize what is truth and what is justice; whereas law is only the application, often imperfectly, of truth and justice in our everyday affairs. The common law of England has been moulded for centuries by lawyers and judges who have been brought up in the Christian faith.

The precepts of religion, consciously or unconsciously, have been their guide in the administration of justice. "If religion perishes in the land, truth and justice will also. We have strayed too far from the faith of our forebears. Let us return to it, for it is the only thing that can save us"[8]

This may seem a grand claim, but part of Denning's genius was to recognise that law should always be the servant of justice and that without religion the foundations upon which justice is built will be no more than shifting sands. **Sands of secularising and pluralising.**

[8] The Rt Hon Lord Denning, *The Influence of Religion on Law*, Sterling Press, Gwent, 1989, pp.33-34

LAW & JUSTICE

A common mistake amongst lawyers and non-lawyers alike is to believe that law and justice are synonymous. As Marlon Brando said about the South African Apartheid regime in the film *A Dry White Season*:

> "Justice and Law [are] distant cousins, and here in South Africa they are not even on speaking terms."

The relationship between law and justice can be an uneasy one – just look at the legal status of slavery at the time of the abolition of the Transatlantic slave trade.

Trading in slaves had been turned into a system of serfdom in England in the early 12th century by virtue of the Magna Carta. Developments over the centuries, if anything, encouraged the trade which had flourished throughout the eighteenth century.

It is interesting to note, however, that Chapters 39 and 40 of the Magna Carta, 1215, echo the Law and the Prophets of the Hebrew Scripture:

> "39. No free man shall be seized or imprisoned or stripped of his rights or possessions, or outlawed or exiled, or deprived of his standing in any other way, nor will we proceed with force against him, or send others to do so, except by the lawful judgement of his equals or by the law of the land.
>
> 40. To no one will we sell, to no one deny or delay right or justice." [9]

And then there are those totalitarian states who by reason of dictatorship, elected or otherwise, or *coup d'état* become places where law and justice walk on opposite sides of the street – parallel lines that stretch far into the distance forever walking apart.

In extreme situations Justice demands that we may use the law in the way it is not intended to achieve a just outcome. During my time in Uganda trying to uphold the rule of law in a country ruled by a dictator, Idi Amin, I once had occasion to send to jail men who were innocent. At first blush this would appear to be the most terrible miscarriage of Justice. Yet outside the court, in Northern Uganda, soldiers had gathered to take these men, if they had been released, and kill them on the orders of the President.

[9] Translated from the Latin by Lord Bingham in his book, *'The Rule of Law'* Allen Lane (2010) p.10

By sending those nine men to jail, and then releasing them two weeks later, when the soldiers were not around, those men were deprived of their liberty for fourteen days, but given their lives. On their release I told them to get out of the country at once.

SO, WHAT IS JUSTICE?

In attempting to find a definition of Justice it's helpful to say first of all what justice isn't - justice isn't simply punishment or retribution. For the true purpose of punishment is penitence.

When people are crying out for vengeance, mistaking it for justice, those ancient words "an eye for an eye, a tooth for a tooth" are trotted out. For me justice was best expressed by the great teacher from Nazareth who said:

> "You have heard that it was said 'An eye for an eye and a tooth for a tooth', But I say to you, do not resist an evil person. If someone strikes you on the right cheek, turn the other also…if someone forces you to go one mile, go also the second mile. (Matthew 5:38-41)."

Tevye, the Fiddler on the Roof, presented his own take on the ancient proposition for vengeance, when he said, "If you insist on carrying out on an eye for an eye and a tooth for a tooth, the whole world will end up totally blind and toothless!"

This practice of citing a mistaken idea of justice in the pursuit for vengeance has often led to miscarriages of justice.

To be redemptive, punishment must be more than removing the perpetrator, permanently or temporarily – it must provide an avenue for total transformation of the situation.

Total restoration means the changing of lives so that the maladies that cause division are eliminated – total transformation based on renewal as was the case in Archbishop Desmond Tutu's *restorative justice* in the South African context; and Nelson Mandela's encouragement of Black people to focus their rage into acts of reconciliation.

This has been powerfully portrayed in the recent film *Invictus.*

In all we do, we need to remember that justice is more than just what goes on in law courts.

The Greeks defined **Justice** as **giving to God and to others that which is their due**. Jesus of Nazareth showed people in his day how to live in such a way that both God and people receive their proper place in our lives.

He showed us how to behave both towards God and towards others:

"In everything, do to others as you would have them do to you" (Matthew 7:12).

And so our hope for creative living in this world house that we have inherited lies in our ability to re-establish the moral ends of our lives in personal character and social justice. Without this spiritual and moral awakening we shall destroy ourselves in the misuse of our own instruments. For justice isn't out there! It isn't without us as a fact, it's within us as a great yearning.

In my judgement liberty and equality are bad principles because they are so hide-bound by individualistic subjectivity.

Which leads me naturally to the story of a jumbo-jet that developed serious engine trouble in mid-Atlantic. The captain told the passengers and asked their permission to open the hold and dump all their luggage in the ocean. "Yes, yes, yes", they all cried. It was done.

Thirty minutes later the captain said, "We are still losing altitude. We must get rid of all your hand luggage. The cabin crew will collect them and when we have dropped to a safer height they will throw them out."

"But of course", the cries went out. And it was done.

An hour later the captain said, "We still need to lose more weight.

Fifty people will be safely dropped into the water with their life-jackets. This airline operates an Inclusive Equal Opportunities Policy. And we shall now put it into operation. We shall use the alphabet to guide us.

A – are there any Africans on board?

Silence

B – are there any Blacks on board?

Silence

C – are there any Caribbeans on board?

Silence.

A little black boy turned to his father and said, "Dad, who are we?"

The father replied, "We are Zulus!"

Liberty and Equality?

The only true principal for humanity is justice, inspired and nourished by love and true compassion; and justice towards the weak becomes necessarily protection or kindness.

And so true peace isn't merely the absence of tension; its the presence of justice.

Justice is important in all walks of life, and lived out to the full, gives hope for the future.

To the freed slaves from Egypt the book of Deuteronomy says,

> "Justice, and only justice, you shall follow, that you may live and inherit the land which the Lord your God gives you" (Deut 16:20). Centuries later prophet Micah was to say to an unjust society.
>
> "He has showed you, O man, what is good; and what does the Lord require of you but to do justice and to love kindness, and to walk humbly with your God" (Micah 6:8).
>
> And for Jesus of Nazareth, "Set your minds on God's kingdom and his justice before everything else, and all the rest will come to you as well" (Matthew 6:33).

The profound and thrilling vibration of justice, the sense of ultimate justice makes the heart suddenly quiver with love. Justice doesn't less exist because her laws are neglected.

In a Secularising and Pluralising Society, justice, to be seen to be done, needs to be **Restorative Justice.**

The definition of restorative justice, increasingly used internationally, emphasises both the process and the outcome:

Restorative justice is a process whereby parties with a stake in a specific offence resolve collectively how to deal with the aftermath of the offence and its implications for the future.[10]

A clearer understanding of what Restorative Justice is comes from Thomas Porter on his short analysis of the power of justice:

[10] T F Marshall *Restorative Justice: An Overview* (London 1999), 5.

"Restorative justice, for me, is more clearly the place where truth, justice, mercy and peace meet; truth is seen as the deep sharing and hearing of other's stories in a way that vindicates and empowers.

As a society, and indeed as a world, we are bound together, and one of the hardest things to do is to deliver restorative justice to the perpetrator and at the same time stand side by side with the victims.

Justice is seen as acknowledgement and restitution and respect for the other. It isn't retributive, but restorative. Mercy recognises that apology and forgiveness are mutually needed for restoration and reconciliation as well as the acknowledgement that is key to justice. Peace becomes a real peace based on right relations".[11]

This model of justice, which some may describe as utopian in its aspiration, is based on a thorough understanding of the differences between retributive justice and restorative justice and the consequences on society that flow from the consequences of each.

The principles of Restorative Justice differ from contemporary criminal justice in several ways.

1. Justice requires that we work to restore those who have been injured. Justice should help victims feel better.
2. Those most directly involved and affected by crime should have the opportunity to participate fully in the response if they wish. Justice must serve the interests of the community as well. The offender should be held accountable for the harm done to the victim and hence to the safety and stability of the community.
3. Justice must deal fairly with offenders. The ideal in a democracy is for people to respect the law and not merely fear it.
4. Government's role is to preserve a just public order, and the community's role is to build and maintain a just peace.
5. stice must seek reintegration of offenders into the community.

All these involve the concepts of:

Responsibility

Respect

[11] Thomas W. Porter - *Restorative Justice: Justice as Peace-building,* Eastern Mennonite University (2003).

Reparation

Reintegration

Restoration

Repentance

Reconciliation

and Forgiveness

And Restorative Justice measures success differently - rather than measuring how much punishment is inflicted, it measures how many sufferings are repaired or prevented.

The ability to rebuild relationships between those who have been damaged by crime, at a domestic level, or by oppression and injustice, depends on the readiness to approach one another as human beings in a more radical, and perhaps more vulnerable and humble way

In dealing with the perpetrators of crime, we need to remember that they are members of our own communities, and in wishing to promote restorative justice, we are also attempting to restore health and life within our communities.

If those who commit offences within a community are removed from it, perhaps never to return, the dislocation that causes can be destructive not only to the future of the offender, but also to the work of the community in a role of restoration.

It is important that we understand this concept as it's the cornerstone upon which any new paradigm of **justice**, be it global or domestic, needs to be built upon.

SO WHAT DOES RESTORATIVE JUSTICE LOOK LIKE?

The essential point about restorative justice is that it isn't about punishment. As Archbishop Desmond Tutu has said in his book:

'No future without Forgiveness':

"It is about the healing of breaches, the redressing of imbalances, the restoration of broken relationships. It seeks to rehabilitate both the victim and the perpetrator, who should be given the opportunity to be reintegrated into the community he or she has injured by his or her offence.

> This is a far more personal approach, which sees the offence as something that has happened to people and whose consequence is a rupture in relationships.
>
> Thus we would claim that justice, restorative justice, is being served when efforts are being made to work for healing, for forgiveness and for reconciliation".[12]

Restorative Justice means that my humanity is caught up, is inextricably bound to, yours. We belong in our natural state of community. It is in many ways the opposite of the Descartian thesis: "I think therefore I am", rather it is "I am because we are". It is in a fundamental understanding of our life and very being, defined not in isolation but in a community of others.

Hence to forgive is not just to be altruistic, it becomes the best form of self-interest. What dehumanises you, inexorably dehumanises me.

We are bound up together, and it's in our own interest that harmony exists. But the hardest thing of all is to deliver **restorative justice** to the perpetrator, and at the same time stand side by side with the victims.

Restorative Justice, therefore, posits a paradigm shift that is best understood NOT by asking the oft-quoted 'three questions': (1) What laws have been broken?, (2) Who did it?, (3) What do they deserve?

But by asking: (1) Who has been hurt?, (2) what are their needs?, (3) Who is obliged to meet their needs?

I remember the story in South Africa of a mother at **The Truth and Reconciliation Commission** hearing about her son's murder. The police officer who had ordered the brutal killing was there, shamefacedly listening to the details of what he and his colleagues had done. At the end the room was quiet.

The chair of the commission, Archbishop Desmond Tutu, asked the woman if she had anything to say to the man who had killed her son.

She responded: "I am very full of sorrow. So I am asking you now – come with me to the place where he died, pick up in your hands some of the dust of the place where his body lay, and feel in your soul what it is to have lost so much. And then I will ask you one thing more. When you have felt my sadness, I want you to do this. I have so much love, and without my

[12] *No Future Without Forgiveness: A Personal Overview of South Africa's Truth and Reconciliation Commission* by Archbishop Desmond Tutu, Rider (2000)

son, that love has nowhere to go. So I am asking you – from now on, you be my son, and I will love you in his place."

MORALS & RELIGION

There are those who would doubtless argue that the twinning of Justice with Religion leads inevitably to some form of theocratic state. May I take this opportunity to assure you that this is not what I have in mind. Rather I believe that in discerning where Justice is to be found there is a need to recognise the place of religion in the road map of the Rule of Law.

The consequential state of affairs is not so much a theocracy but rather what developed under the common law, a place where the rule of law is founded upon an understanding of the wider principles of the Judeo-Christian tradition as the tapestry upon which this country's law and values has been weaved.

Without wishing to appear syncretistic or patronizing, in my experience and friendships I have seen that these are values that are also held dear in the traditions of Judaism, Hinduism, Islam, Sikhism, Buddhism and also amongst those who say they have no religious belief, but are people of good will, who are just and truthful in their dealings with their fellow human-beings.

Such values are distinctly religious not because they seek to proselytise or convert, but rather because they are grounded in a moral world view rather than in a shifting relativism of secularism and pluralism.

When it comes to considering the operation of morals within the law, two views of standards are common: for ease of shorthand I would label one as the relativist approach and the other the absolutist viewpoint.

As John Montgomery notes in the conclusion of his keynote address *'Human Dignity in Birth and Death: A Question of Values'*, for the relativist, standards do not exist as moral absolutes over against the human decision-maker. The law serves itself alone and justice occurs only through the administration of the law. Morals have little place in such a view and are replaced instead by a changing set of ethics.[13]

[13] Invitational keynote address at the Conference on Legal and Ethical Issues (Edmonton, 2–4 May 1990), sponsored by the Alberta Hospital Association, the Legal Education Society of Alberta, the Health Law Section of the Canadian Bar Association .

The problem immediately arises as to which set of ethics do we apply? Those in favour of Contextual ethics would argue one way whilst those supporting Existential ethics would argue a different approach.

Those, like Joseph Fletcher, who advocate situational ethics, simply say we should act in love, letting the end justify the means, and not think that the same moral rules are binding everywhere or for all time.

But is not ethical absolutism rigid and unfeeling? It can be, but this need not be the case. In the world of human fragility, transience, corruption, shame and pollution, even when moral issues are clearly seen, one must often face genuine conflicts of principle and the necessity of choosing a lesser of evils.

And while at the same time heeding the timeless warning of Christopher Dawson, who wrote in 1943, when the United Kingdom and the United States of America were in a ferocious war against the great evil of Nazism, saying, "As soon as men decide that all means are permitted to fight an evil, then their good becomes indistinguishable from the evil that they set out to destroy."[14]

Such decisions must not become compromises. They ought to be a mature recognition of the problems inherent in a world divided by differences of language, tribe, nationality, ethnicity, colour, religion and wealth. Here, particularly, the theology represented by classical Christianity can be an incalculable boon, for at its heart God is sharing in our human predicament, and offering forgiveness and hope as we struggle in the slough of ethical ambiguity, striving to apply sound principles to exceedingly complex and often heart-rending individual cases. But always holding on to the truth that human beings are of infinite worth, simply because they are human and not because of any external circumstances or usefulness.

RELIGION & JUSTICE

In his judgement in the recent case involving the News of the World and Sir Max Moseley, Mr. Justice Eady spoke of the "new rights-based jurisprudence" of the Human Rights Act and its operation upon Press Freedoms.

The question of Human Rights, how they can be defended, not so much against invasion by the media but through the desires of Governments to

[14] C Dawson, *'The Judgement of the Nations'*, Sheed and Ward, London, 1943, p.8

circumvent them, is a constant battle and one in which I believe religion plays a central role in its intermingling of law and morals.

Carol Iannone has written a review of *The Clash of Orthodoxies: Law, Religion, and Morality in Crisis* by Robert P. George, the former professor of Jurisprudence at Princeton, in which he suggests that at the heart of this battle is the basic question of 'Why should anyone respect the rights of others?'[15] Merely prudential answers - such as, people should respect the rights of others so that others will respect their rights, or people should respect the rights of others to avoid being punished - simply won't do.

The fact is that people can often get away with violating others' rights.

And they know it. And many do it. If people shouldn't violate the rights of others, it must be because doing so is morally wrong, but on the non-religious account why is it morally wrong? What is the source of its moral wrongness? No satisfactory answer is forthcoming.

None, I submit, is possible. After all, there are no atheists in a fox-hole. For those brutal people who slice off women's breasts or soak their victims in acid know that it is not good for their victims, and that is why they do it!

While the non-religious person stands shakily on slippery ground, searching for foundations they probably would not acknowledge even if they could find them, Professor Robert George argues that "free choice, rationally motivated action, and objective moral truth . . . point beyond themselves to a more-than-merely-human source of meaning and value, a divine ground of human intelligence and free will."[16] Yes, a transcendent source, a revelation to be sure, but one that can be tested, affirmed, and chosen by human reason. The absence of proof is no proof of absence.

In his book Professor Robert George aims to puncture the notion that secular liberalism is merely a matter of tolerance and procedure, possessing no substantive vision of its own. He shows instead how it is actually based on definite, if faulty, ideas about human nature and human life, and how under the guise of its supposed neutrality, it is aggressively imposing its vision on the rest of us. A second goal of this book is to refute the idea that matters of religious morality are derived from faith and therefore have no place in a liberal society dedicated (supposedly) to rational discourse.

While Professor George would surely admit that revelation-based dogmas such as the Trinity have no place in civic discussion, he argues

15 *The Clash of* **Orthodoxies Robert P George, ISI Books , Wilmington, Del.** pp 37-38
16 ***ibid***

persuasively that religiously based morality governing human action is not only reasonable, but more reasonable than its secular counterpart.

THE RE-INTERPRETING OF LAW, RELIGION & MORALS

It is my belief that we need to find a way in which religion, morals and law are once again inextricably intermingled. We can see examples of how this might operate if we take the area of family law as a paradigm.

I would like to illustrate this with the example of a family law dispute from Hebrew Scriptures, The judgement of King Solomon found in 1 Kings Chapter 3 verses 16-28.

Many of you will be familiar with the story of the two women, both of whom claim to be the mother of a child, who come before King Solomon who unfortunately does not have access to DNA technology in arriving at his decision! Solomon calls for a sword and suggests that the way to solve the situation is for neither woman to have the child and to cut the baby in two and for each woman to be given half. Not a tactic I would commend o any of you planning on a future career as family lawyers. The true mother of the child immediately calls for the baby to be given to the other mother at which point King Solomon decides that it was the woman who was prepared to forfeit her own rights for the well being of the child who must be the true mother, whilst the woman who was not the true parent was apparently ready to take the half of a child offered to her.

I believe that in most cases of divorce most parents are like the true mother of the child who stood before King Solomon. The role of the court must be to enable that love and desire for the child's best interest present within both parents, so as to reach that arrangement where the hopes of the parents and the future of the child come together. Sadly the love of one parent bears no fruit when custody is given to one parent and access is severely restricted to the other parent.

Not to take into account the love of one of the parents is like using a sword to cut into half the couple's love for the child.

The hopes of the parents and the future and well-being of the child would come together in divorce proceedings if all parties and the courts, acknowledged the law, acknowledged the wrongdoing of both parties, but also included justice and equity rooted in compassion and humanity.

Religion, Morality and Law were once intermingled. This intermingling helped to shape both the Common Law and the Statutes of this land, and in all Nations of the former British Empire. It also greatly influenced the way in which the judges interpreted the law.

As I have already said, above, the law is now regarded purely as an instrument for regulating our personal affairs – completely severed from morality and religion. Like Lord Denning, I believe that such severance has gone too far.

It is my belief that we urgently need to reaffirm, fan into flame, and live those values which we owe to the Christian legacy. Law, Religion and Morals, once again inter-mingled.

I believe this will reinvigorate citizenship and the renewal of a just society, brilliantly presented by Professor Michael Sandel – Professor of Government at Harvard University, BBC Reith Lecturer 2009 - in his moral philosophy, *'Justice, What's the Right Thing to Do?'* [17]

Finally, let me conclude by saying that my thesis chimes in with Tom Bingham's examination of the meaning of *'The Rule of Law'*

Tom Bingham, the outstanding British judge of the past quarter-century – a master of the judicial art, and one of the world's most acute legal minds, in his timely book, makes clear that the rule of Law is not an arid legal doctrine but is the foundation of a fair and just society, a guarantee of responsible government, and an important contribution to economic growth, as well as offering the best means yet devised for securing peace and co-operation. He advocates eight conditions which capture its essence as understood in Western democracies today.

He ends by saying that,

> "The rule of law is one of the greatest unifying factors, perhaps the greatest, the nearest we are likely to approach to a universal secular religion. It remains an ideal, but an ideal worth striving for, in the interests of good government and peace, at home and in the world at large."[18]

Justice in a Secularising and Pluralising Society cries out for the intermingling, once again, of Law, Religion and Morals.

Thank you for listening.

[17] Michael J Sandel, *'Justice', What's the Right Thing to do?'* Penguin Books, London, 2009

[18] Tom Bingham, *'The Rule of Law'*, Allen Lane, Penguin Books, London, 2010, p.174

Legal Issues Facing the United Nations

PATRICIA O'BRIEN

Under-Secretary for Legal Affairs at the United Nations

15 November 2010

I NTRODUCTION

It is a great pleasure and an honour to address you this evening. I see this not only as a personal compliment but as an indication of your interest in the work of the United Nations and in international law.

Last year, when I was bestowed with the honour of becoming a Bencher of this noble I nn of Court, I was invited to spend some time with you and to speak about issues facing us in the UN, I did not hesitate to accept. The challenge we faced was to find a mutually convenient date. Thank you, Master Treasurer and Lord Justice Burnton, for your patience. With the peripatetic life I lead, I have begun to feel that this beautiful Hall is part of my home.

BACKGROUND

It is just over two years since I joined the UN as Legal Counsel to head the Office of Legal Affairs. I thought I would start by giving you some background to my role: Before I took up the post, my main experience of the organisation was as the I rish Foreign Ministry's legal adviser. I n many respects, I was an outsider- from a small but committed member state - looking in on how this vast and complex body worked. Naturally, this only allowed for a fleeting glimpse at most of the issues, or, for a very concentrated focus on an issue of particular national importance. I n my role as Legal Adviser of the UN, I now have a clear sense of how centrally international law currently figures among UN priorities.

The Office of Legal Affairs employs about 200 staff on a full-time basis and acts as in-house Counsel to the Secretary-General, to the senior management and to the wider UN system. Much of our work is, understandably, carried out quietly and behind the scenes. We cover a range of issues of international public law which many people would associate with the UN – for example, advice on the law applicable to war, Peacekeeping Operations, Oceans & international criminal justice, contracts of over $4 billion, procurement matters, Treaty Law, privileges and immunities, international trade law/UNCITRAL and the new system of administration of justice for a staff of more than 60,000.

The Charter of the UN is, of course, the fundamental and primary law of the UN.

So to the Charter: where the Peoples of the UN expressed their determination *"to establish conditions under which justice and respect for the obligations arising from treaties and other sources of international law can be maintained"*. Since 1945, the Organization and its Members have constantly striven to give practical meaning to this resolve and to develop legal bases for peaceful relations between States. My Office plays a central role assisting states in the negotiation of Treaties and international legal texts which have become milestones in the field.

Over the years, the UN has seen periods of great advancement in international law and jurisprudence, just as there have been times when our function as guardian of the global legal architecture has seemed more peripheral. Since joining the Organisation, it has become clear to me that international law - and the role of the UN as its champion - is absolutely central to the work of the UN and to the Secretary-General and his team. The Secretary-General places a particular emphasis on the need to reform the administration of the UN and to manage the resources of the Organization as effectively as possible including minimizing duplication and overlap. We - as lawyers - are at the Secretary-General's table on so many issues at his Policy Committee; Senior Management Group; which I suppose one could liken most closely to a cabinet, and which meets every week; and his Management and Political Advisory meetings, etc.

My meetings with the Secretary-General occur on a frequent basis for one reason or another- often, for instance, on issues of public international law but also for issues relating to the administration and management of the UN. Discussions at all the Secretary-General's meetings, as you might imagine, are lively and sometimes difficult. As chair, the Secretary-General works to ensure that the focus remains firmly on his goals for the Organization.

As Legal Counsel, among my tasks is to support the Secretary-General's commitment to the strengthening of the rule of law, the pursuit of justice and the determination to end impunity for genocide, crimes against humanity, war crimes and other serious violations of international humanitarian and human rights law. So I will focus on this topic which, in one way or another, permeates my activities on a daily basis.

My Office plays a key role in promoting the rule of law at the national and international levels. Many people see references to the rule of law as little more than the high-blown rhetoric of international conferences attended by people who do not live in the real world where the rule of law is constantly under threat or indeed, in some cases, is non-existent. Others view the rule of law, while well-intentioned, as falling firmly into the category of abstract conceptual theory.

However, the pursuit of this principle is a recognition that, without it, the lines between justice and tyranny can too easily blur or disappear altogether. We witness the results of its absence on a daily basis in so many countries. Quite frankly, its promotion and protection is a goal which permeates all our work at the Office of Legal Affairs. Establishing respect for the rule of law is fundamental and essential for a number of reasons, including: prevention of conflict; achieving a durable peace in the aftermath of conflict; the effective protection of human rights; and also, of course, sustained economic progress and development.

The principle of the rule of law, embedded in the Charter, encompasses elements relevant to the conduct of state to state relations. I n addition to the I CJ, the main UN organs including the General Assembly and the Security Council, all have essential roles in this regard. The principle that everyone is accountable to the law -from the individual to the State itself-is, of course, a fundamental concept which drives much of our work.

THE FIGHT AGAINST IMPUNITY AND THE AGE OF ACCOUNTABILITY

I have decided to focus on accountability and our ongoing quest to end impunity for genocide, crimes against humanity, war crimes and other violations of international humanitarian and human rights law.

At the recent Review Conference of the ICC held in Kampala which I attended with the Secretary-General, he recalled that the international community had overwhelmingly embraced "an Age of Accountability".

He stressed this again in his annual address to the General Assembly in September. He emphasised in Kampala that impunity for international crimes is no longer an option, as shown by the developments which followed the conflicts in Rwanda, the former Yugoslavia, Sierra Leone, Cambodia and elsewhere. He constantly looks to what more can be done to achieve justice.

International criminal mechanisms have already achieved a great deal. A number of those who, from high positions, planned and directed the most serious crimes in the conflicts I have just mentioned have been brought to justice or are currently facing trial. Heads of State have not been exempted. Before the establishment of these mechanisms, impunity was viewed by some perpetrators of terrible crimes as a very likely outcome. This is no longer the case. At the same time, the international community cannot be complacent. Unfortunately, to date, only a relatively small number of those responsible for genocide, crimes against humanity or war crimes find themselves before a court of law. Their victims have rarely been granted redress for the unimaginable suffering they endured.

The panoply of international and mixed tribunals established by the UN since the mass atrocities in the former Yugoslavia and Rwanda in the early to mid-1990s began with the I nternational Criminal Tribunals for the former Yugoslavia and for Rwanda. These were followed by the Extraordinary Chambers for Cambodia, the Special Court for Sierra Leone and the Special Tribunal for Lebanon. For almost two decades, international criminal tribunals have contributed to the gradual erosion of impunity and the prosecution of those responsible in political and military leadership roles for commission of serious, large-scale crimes. These international judicial mechanisms have been at the heart of the revival and development of international criminal law and jurisprudence.

The ICC is the centrepiece of our system of international criminal justice. If we want to be serious about combating impunity and nurturing and developing a culture of accountability, we must support its work.

Despite the understandable challenges which the I CC is facing in consolidating itself as a vital and indispensable part of the community of international organizations, I firmly believe that where states are unable or unwilling to investigate and prosecute, the I CC is our main hope in the quest to end impunity for international crimes.

This Court provides the opportunity and the vehicle for our generation to significantly advance the cause of justice and, in so doing, to reduce and prevent unspeakable suffering. I f we fail to support the I CC, we fail humanity.

Complementarity

It is clear that the UN has a responsibility to support the I CC and to spearhead the international effort to bring justice for these crimes. And we take that responsibility seriously. However, I take every opportunity to emphasise the role of States. The principle of complementarity is essentially the duty of States first and foremost to prosecute international crimes. Only where national judicial systems are unable or unwilling to investigate or prosecute should international courts be involved. This principle is of crucial importance for the future of international criminal justice and the quest to end impunity for grave violations. This issue of complementarity is at the heart of much of our current work.

We are all aware that international justice mechanisms, whether permanent or ad hoc, are not intended to supplant States where they have organized criminal justice systems which are willing and able to ensure that there is accountability for the crimes concerned.

International mechanisms are not substitutes for national mechanisms.

The premise of the complementarity principle is that national systems are best placed to investigate and prosecute the statutory crimes of the Rome Statute. I t is national systems which are closest to the victims and affected communities. The preference for national judicial proceedings is at the heart of the Rome Statute/I CC system.

If we want to remain on the offensive in our quest to end impunity and to ensure the prospects for a genuine "Age of Accountability", we must be truly committed to strengthening national judicial capacities. I believe that the full potential of a proactive approach to complementarity is far from realized.

The UN can and will assist States with technical cooperation and rule of law support. But again it will, first and foremost, be up to States to embrace and implement the principle of complementarity.

In the final analysis, justice is a nation's choice. The fight against impunity cannot be won at the international level alone. I t must be fought and won inside States, with the political will of the Governments and in the hearts and minds of the citizens. Supporting the principle of complementarity through fortifying national judicial systems is a priority in our common fight against impunity for the coming years.

National systems must assume a more prominent role in filling the impunity gap that currently exists in dealing with international crimes.

Tribunals

The building of a culture of accountability is a challenge that the UN and the Secretary-General has vigorously undertaken. As I mentioned, many important trials against perpetrators of international crimes in the former Yugoslavia and in Rwanda have been conducted by the I CTY and the I CTR, the Special Court for Sierra Leone and the Extraordinary Chambers in the Courts of Cambodia. Work is ongoing at the Special Tribunal for Lebanon to bring to trial those responsible for the assassination of President Rafiq Hariri.

The Tribunals have taken important steps to develop international criminal law.

The Special Court for Sierra Leone was the first "mixed" or "hybrid" Tribunal established by Agreement between the UN and a State. This Court is now winding down its presence in Sierra Leone. I t has handed over its jail to the government which is now using it as a women's prison. The Court handed down its final verdict in Freetown in November last year. The Court's only remaining trial - the case against Liberian former President Charles Taylor is currently ongoing. So the Court is preparing to close its doors after a successful undertaking (estimated to close June 2013). I t will be the first international Tribunal to end its work.

A breakthrough has recently been achieved in the context of the Court of Cambodia (ECCC) with (i) the historic arrest and surrender of five principal Khmer Rouge leaders to the Court; (ii) the successful completion of the first trial; and (iii) the recent indictment of the five leaders. This Court has become a catalyst for strengthening the rule of law in Cambodia. Unlike the other UN-assisted courts, it is not an international tribunal, but a court embedded in the national jurisdiction of Cambodia. I t is a national court with participation by international judges, prosecutors and administrators.

The Court has recently successfully completed its first trial. On 26 July 2010, the Court convicted Kaing Guek Eav, alias Duch, of crimes against humanity, grave breaches of the Geneva Conventions, and serious offences under Cambodian national law. There has been criticism that the sentence of 35 years was too light. But, this is a topic of its own. I t is one which is mirrored in so many national jurisdictions and, in my view, this discussion now in Cambodia is evidence itself of the evolution of the rule of law within the

State. Duch was the Secretary of the 521 detention centre in Phnom Penh, where records show that more than 12,000 people were detained and executed, although the actual numbers are believed to have been considerably greater.

One of the really striking successes of the ECCC is the impact it has had on Cambodian society. More than 31,000 Cambodians visited the ECCC to witness the proceedings against Duch, many travelling long distances from the provinces and staying overnight. This number is believed to be higher than for any of the other UN-assisted tribunals. I t is a forceful reminder of the importance of pursuing justice in the country where atrocities have taken place wherever possible. Further, there is a strong potential for the transfer of capacity and international standards to the national courts since the ECCC is embedded in Cambodia's national court structure and jurisdiction, with participation by international and Cambodian judges, prosecutors and court administrators. When I visited the ECCC in April this year, and again two weeks ago I was struck by the determination and professionalism of the national judges and officials. Cambodia is serious about the need to ensure that new skills and standards are retained, and that the rule of law in Cambodia is enhanced.

The ECCC is likely to prosecute a relatively limited number of the senior leaders of the former Khmer Rouge regime and those most responsible for the shocking crimes that took place in Cambodia in the 1970s. This Court will also therefore complete its work in the next few years. The Court is not just a mechanism for accountability, bringing justice to the victims of the Khmer Rouge regime. Equally important is the fact that, in a country like Cambodia, it is also a catalyst for its national judicial reform and development, and has become an essential element of building capacity for the establishment of rule of law and good governance.

ESTABLISHMENT OF RESIDUAL MECHANISMS

The fact that most of these UN-assisted tribunals are approaching the completion of their work is not the end of the story. The tribunals have a number of essential functions which must continue beyond the lifespan of the tribunals themselves. These include: (i) the trial of any fugitives- it is imperative that fugitives are not allowed to avoid justice by "out-waiting" the tribunals; (ii) the protection of witnesses; (iii) the international monitoring of the enforcement of prison sentences; and (iv) the archives of the tribunals must continue to be properly managed.

The bodies to succeed each of the UN-assisted tribunals have become known as "residual mechanisms". These successor bodies will in fact be courts - naturally smaller and leaner successors to their judicial predecessors. The challenge will be to design these mechanisms so that they are able to carry out the residual functions that I have just listed, including the judicial, prosecutorial and administrative aspects of those functions, with limited staff and resources.

The issues, both legal and administrative, are novel and complex.

In designing, negotiating and establishing these residual mechanisms, the UN Office of Legal Affairs is at the forefront of developing the future architecture of international criminal justice to complement that of the I CC. The Office of Legal Affairs is the lead department in the UN for the tribunals and their successor bodies. I t falls to us to ensure that the residual mechanism can commence functioning at the very moment that the tribunal is terminated, with continuity of jurisdiction and a smooth passing of the residual functions.

Questions abound as to the effect of justice on prevention of atrocities and punishment - R2P

Many of you will be familiar with the extreme violence that has occurred in more recent times in places as diverse as Afghanistan, Darfur, the Democratic Republic of the Congo, Guinea, Kyrgyzstan and Sri Lanka. The topic of ending impunity has thus not gone away and becomes ever more acute. I n many of these places and situations, the targeting of civilians, sexual violence, forced displacement and denial of humanitarian access are acts which, more often than not, have been carried out with impunity.

The UN is best placed to lead the international effort to put an end to such violence. But the response to global violence must, of course, be the joint effort of States, non-State entities, international organizations both governmental and non-governmental and civil society at large. The question at the centre of the debate is: how to prevent the violence and to punish those responsible for its consequences. However, in the practice of the international community, including the UN, prevention and punishment which are of course "two distinct yet connected obligations" have (in the words of the I CJ in the Genocide case) -too often been seen as "punishment as prevention". One of the most effective ways of preventing criminal acts, according to many great legal philosophers and jurists, is to provide penalties and to impose them effectively on persons who committed them. But while punishment as a deterrence or a form of prevention has been a common purpose of all international criminal jurisdictions -one, among many - in reality, punishment alone and the prospect of it seldom prevents. Clearly, prevention requires much more.

I believe the core idea that has inspired the UN action in the field of human rights and humanitarian law is that compliance with relevant rules is a matter of concern to the international community as a whole. Such compliance will prevent these crimes. I nternational law powerfully mirrors this idea, when it conveys that, while the primary responsibility for complying with international humanitarian and human rights law falls upon the State directly involved, the international community also has a role to play to ensure respect for the law. This is the same conviction that brought the 2005 World Summit to proclaim the concept of the "Responsibility to Protect", which provides that "[e]ach individual State has the responsibility to protect its populations from genocide, war crimes, ethnic cleansing and crimes against humanity" and that "[t]he international community, through the United Nations, also has the responsibility ... to help to protect populations from" those crimes. The focus is on prevention of these crimes and protection of civilians must be a corollary of protection.

The concept of R2P is a powerful notion that has attracted the attention both of Governments and the international legal community. We have identified three pillars for advancing the World Summit's landmark decision in this area: Pillar One on the responsibility of States to protect their own population; Pillar Two on "I nternational assistance and capacity-building" to assist States to protect their population; and Pillar Three on a "Timely and decisive response" by the international community where States are not able or willing to protect their population.

Interestingly, the notion of an "international rule of law", which -I believe lies at the heart of the responsibility to protect, may again prove useful in understanding the action needed under these three pillars of R2P.

Under the first pillar, there is a need for States to become parties to relevant international instruments on human rights, I HL and refugee law, and to the I CC Statute; and the core international standards need to be faithfully embodied in national legislation. The presence of a strong culture of rule of law in a society may prevent or minimize the risk of deterioration into an "R2P" situation.

Under the second pillar, there is a need for assistance programmes to build specific capacities within societies that would make them less likely to travel the path to crimes relating to the responsibility to protect.

Under the third pillar, emphasis is needed on all the available tools provided under the Charter, notably in Chapters VI , VI I and VI I I . This confirms that our goal is not to add a new layer of bureaucracy, or to re-label existing United Nations programmes; it is to incorporate the responsibility to protect as a perspective into ongoing efforts, including those on the promotion of the rule of law. The discussion on a strategy to implement the responsibility to protect is still ongoing, but the concept shows the potential benefits that a unified action in this field may bring to the international community as a whole.

TARGETED SANCTIONS

Now I wish to briefly turn to the issue of sanctions which has recently resurfaced after the European General Court rendered its decision in the second round of the so-called "Kadi" jurisprudence on 30 September:

The issue is that of fair and clear procedures for the Security Council sanctions regime. It is an issue which has the potential to cause significant tensions for States in their commitments to the UN and regional organisations to which they belong.

The issue itself is as old as the invention of "smart" or "targeted sanctions".

It exists ever since the Security Council began moving towards imposing targeted sanctions with respect to particular individuals and entities, rather than imposing comprehensive sanctions with respect to governments or trade sectors. This shift has resulted in making sanctions more effective, and focussing the effects where they belong. Such sanctions usually involve the imposition of travel bans, the freezing of assets and arms embargoes.

In light of the increasing number of persons who are subject to such measures in the context of counter-terrorism activities, targeted sanctions raise a number of concerns, in particular as to how human rights and fundamental freedoms of persons who are subject to such sanctions can be respected.

The Secretary-General, pursuant to this mandate, took the initiative to convey his views on this issue to the Members of the Security Council in 2006.

He submitted to the Council that minimum standards, required to ensure fair and clear procedures, would have to include several basic elements, including the right to be informed; the right to be heard; the right to be assisted or represented by counsel; and the right to review by an effective review mechanism.

Security Council resolutions of 2005 and 2006 have improved the notification of listings. A further resolution in 2008 aimed to address the issue of the right to be heard.

In December 2009, the Security Council unanimously adopted Resolution 1904 (2009) in an effort to address the right to an effective review mechanism.

Most notably, the Council decided to establish the "Office of the Ombudsperson" to assist the "1267 Committee" when it considers delisting requests from individuals and entities. For the first time, petitioners seeking their removal from the list can present their case to an independent and impartial Ombudsperson who, after consultations with both relevant states and the petitioner will present his observations to the Committee. I n the words of the Council, the creation of this role addresses the "right to review by an independent mechanism."

We will have to see how the first Ombudsperson implements her important mandate and how the interaction between the Ombudsperson and the Committee on the one hand, and between the Ombudsperson and the petitioners works in practice. Eventually, a lot will also depend on how the Ombudsperson's observations will be taken up and dealt with by the Committee.

The UN Office of Legal Affairs welcomed all of these steps taken towards ensuring fair and clear procedures for placing individuals and entities on Security Council sanctions lists and for removing them. These positive developments are a reflection of a widely shared perception that progress was needed.

Meanwhile, however, these developments have been accompanied by a growing number of court cases around the world, in which listed individuals and entities have challenged their listing. They have argued that their fundamental human rights have been infringed due to the lack of adequate procedures provided by the Security Council sanctions regime. A corresponding national and regional jurisprudence emerges.

In fact, in addition to the Kadi case, several national and regional courts have been seized of cases which concern, inter alia, obligations under coercive measures issued by the Security Council under Chapter VI I of the Charter and their compatibility with obligations under international law, and, specifically for European States, with obligations arising under the European Convention for the Protection of Human Rights and Fundamental Freedoms.

We are following these cases with great interest and concern. There are more cases currently before the Court of Justice of the European Union and, in particular, before the General Court. The Kadi case is certainly the leading case in many respects and we are all following its progress closely.

PIRACY

Now - for a wholly different flavour of our work: I will speak briefly about Piracy. For my Office, the piracy dossier is an active and important one. The human cost of piracy off the coast of Somalia is incalculable, with killings and widespread hostage-taking of sailors whose daily jobs are already filled with risk. The commercial cost is also very high. The problem clearly demonstrates the increasing interdependence of States and people in a globalised world. The number and diversity of States and organisations with a stake in finding a solution provides strong evidence of this, with human welfare, and commercial and security interests under threat.

Piracy has a rather technical definition in the United Nations Convention on the Law of the Sea (UNCLOS). Essentially it includes violence or detention for private ends by the crew of a private ship against another ship. I t is not a complex crime. Some refer to it colloquially as "robbery at sea, although, of course it is broader than this, and includes hostage-taking, which has had such a devastating effect on the lives of so many.

As piracy is a crime which, by definition takes place on the high seas, beyond the territorial jurisdiction of any State, UNCLOS and customary international law provide for universal jurisdiction over it. Any State may seize a pirate ship, arrest and detain the perpetrators, and prosecute them. There is no lack of international law for dealing with piracy, but rather a lack of implementation. Over the last few years, however, the international naval presence off the coast of Somalia and the arrangements between some naval States and regional States for transfer and prosecution of suspects, has begun to have an impact. The number of piracy incidents is still high, but the effectiveness of these attacks has been diminishing each year. The efforts of Kenya and the Seychelles in particular to conduct prosecutions is commendable. One of our key efforts must be to try to encourage and assist an increase in the number of such regional States to play an active role.

The measures which the international community put in place to combat the problem have demonstrated the strengths of the legal regime established under UNCLOS, but also the regime's reliance on States with the capacity and political will to fully implement its provisions. A number of entities within the UN and the I nternational Maritime Organization have been engaged in efforts to assist States in addressing the legal issues which emerge from the apprehension, detention and prosecution of suspected pirates.

The Secretary-General has been the driving force behind these UN efforts. On 25 August, he introduced a report to the Security Council in which he identifies seven possible options to further the aim of prosecuting and imprisoning those responsible. The knowledge and experience that the Office of Legal Affairs has developed of international tribunals over the past two decades placed us very well to prepare this report on behalf of the Secretary General. For the Security Council, I set out the international legal regime and details of the seven options. These include the creation of special domestic chambers in regional States, possibly with participation by international judges and prosecutors; a regional tribunal; or an international tribunal on the lines of the former Yugoslavia and Rwanda tribunals, and corresponding imprisonment arrangements.

The Secretary-General's report was welcomed as an important and timely contribution, and food for thought for the Security Council. I t is critical that the international community does not tolerate impunity for crimes of piracy. However, as recognised in the report, piracy is a symptom of the instability that has persisted in Somalia for nearly two decades. Prosecution of those responsible must therefore form part of an integrated international response which aims to help rebuild the rule of law, and economic and social stability on land in Somalia.

CONCLUSION

Ladies and Gentlemen, Colleagues,

With this I have reached the end of my remarks tonight.

Thank you for listening to this address on a wide range of issues. I 'm sure you noted that the issues addressed ranged from a very old problem, piracy, to the responsibility to protect, a concept that was formulated in those terms only in recent years.

This range of issues reflects well the broader practice of the Office of Legal Affairs in New York, which confronts on any given day issues arising in core areas of our practice that date back to the days of the UN Charter and cutting edge issues that may be drawn from the headlines of the day.

I hope that I have succeeded in conveying to you the dynamic quality of the practice of international law at the United Nations, a feature of its practice which is, of course, shared with many other intergovernmental organizations, national government legal adviser's offices, and non-governmental organizations.

It is in light of this dynamic quality that I believe that it is a very good time for a law student to be considering becoming an international lawyer. The challenges that such a career presents and the satisfactions that such a career produces are substantial. I encourage your continued interest in the practice of international law.

I would be grateful for comments and thoughts that you may have at this point. And I will try my best to answer any questions that you may have.

Thank you very much.

The Rule of Law & Global Terrorism - An International Problem from a Northern Irish Perspective

MARK MULHOLLAND,Q.C.

Chairman of the General Council of the Bar of Northern Ireland and Chairman of the Executive Council of the Inn of Court of Northern Ireland

18 December 2012

INTRODUCTION

I am deeply honoured to have been asked to give this year's international Rule of Law lecture. I would like to thank Michael and Chantal in particular for the very kind invitation for which I am truly humbled. I would also like to express my sincere appreciation to Sarah Richardson and Natalie Darby from the Bar Council of England and Wales for all their very kind help and able assistance.

It was an Irish barrister of some renown, John Philpott Curran, MP and later Master of the Rolls, who provides the context for the theme of tonight's lecture on the International Rule of Law. At it's very heart – 'eternal vigilance'. For it was Curran, who, long before the phrase was attributed to Thomas Jefferson in 1838 or Andrew Jackson the preceding year, in a speech he gave in 1790 upon the right of election, extolled the virtue,

> "It is the common fate of the indolent to see their rights become a prey to the active. The condition upon which God hath given liberty to man is eternal vigilance ; which condition if he break, servitude is at once the consequence of his crime and the punishment of his guilt".

The UK threat level regarding terrorist attack is currently assessed to be 'substantial', meaning an attack is a strong possibility. Protection of the public is paramount, and 222 years on, 'eternal vigilance' remains the price of democracy and freedom. But the practical meaning of 'eternal vigilance' can be open to interpretation or some may even say, lost in translation, depending upon which arm of the State to which we are referring.

The Home Office quarterly update to June 2012, released just last week, shows that arrests for suspected terrorism offences rose by 60% in the last year.

The dichotomy between Executive and Judicial functions are at the very heart of our democratic system – whilst the Government may construe eternal vigilance to mean the protection of the public at all cost, the fundamental role of the independent judiciary is in underpinning the necessity at the same time in maintaining and ensuring that the rule of law is observed by the Government in the measures that may be necessary in their eyes to bring terrorists to justice.

As once observed by Lord Judge, it is the judges 'who are the guardians of the rule of law'. That is their prime responsibility and in real terms, eternal vigilance by the judiciary means that they are steadfastly alert for the 'first incursion by the executive into propriety'.

This is the 6th lecture on the International Rule of Law – I am disinclined to give you its 6th interpretation - Joseph Raz in 'The Rule of Law and its Virtue' talks of the "promiscuous use" made in recent years of the expression the rule of law. This concept of promiscuity I must confess intrigued me …

'Berlusconi, Bunga bunga & the Rule of Law' – that's the 7th Annual lecture taken care of!

Certainly stripping it all away... no pun intended.. Joseph Raz, writing in 1977, states that a core principle of the rule of law is, 'the independence of the judiciary must be guaranteed', which remains as true today as it did then. This lies at the very heart of all we may consider this evening.

It is against the backdrop of eternal vigilance and the role of the judiciary that I will embark on our journey into 'Global Terrorism and the Rule of Law – an International problem from a Northern Irish perspective'.

The theme of this talk is to look at the rule of law and its application to the Government's response to terrorism both nationally and internationally and to see what lessons can be learned through the Northern Ireland experience, spanning over the past four decades.

i. This will examine the transition from the beginning of the troubles in 1969, the Government response through measures such as internment, Diplock trials, confession only convictions, the use of the supergrass system and the allegations of collusion - up to and including the de Silva report.

ii. It will consider the vital role played by the legal profession in Northern Ireland, the work of the independent Bar and the constant threat endured by the judiciary.

iii. It will further consider the lessons to be learned underpinning the necessity of maintaining and ensuring that the rule of law is observed by the Government in the measures that may be viewed as expedient or necessary in dealing with terrorism in a national and international context.

iv. It will examine some of the cardinal principles that underpin the international rule of law in this context, the role of the European Court of Human Rights and address the criticisms of judicial decisions taken in recent high profile cases such as that of Abu Qatada by the media and Government.

v. Finally it will look to other legal jurisdictions to examine the lessons that can be learned in the transition to a 'post conflict society' and the necessity of a robust and independent legal profession and judiciary in getting to that point, thus ensuring the rule of law is observed into the future.

So let's go back to the past before we look to the future...

It was Winston Churchill, at the close of the Great War remarking on the entrenched views of those in Northern Ireland, spoke of how,

> "...the whole map of Europe has been changed. The position of countries has been violently altered...but as the deluge subsides and the waters fall short, we see the dreary steeples of Fermanagh and Tyrone emerging once again. The integrity of their quarrel is one of the few institutions that has been unaltered in the cataclysm which has swept the world."

The Great War a century later has now been replaced by a global war – spanning the borders of Europe and beyond. The horrors of trench warfare have been replaced internationally with calls for 'holy jihad' and suicide bombings. The 9/11 report details countering terrorism as the top national priority, as we all know to be the 'War on terror'. Fought on both a national and international stage by the US and its allies.

How you may ask do the Churchillian dreary steeples of Fermanagh and Tyrone have anything to do with Al Qaeda, global terrorism and the international rule of law?

The response to terrorism whether nationally or globally must be viewed through the prism of the fundamental principles enshrined in the Rule of Law - the lessons to be learned in the modern day state's response to terrorism, its efficacy, lawfulness and effectiveness can be considered in the context of Northern Ireland, which provides for the ideal backdrop, given that 'the state has been in a condition of permanent emergency' since its inception' in 1921.

Certainly the conflict in NI and the 'integrity of their quarrel' in NI, have been all too painfully aware...

I had been born in 1969, three months after British soldiers arrived onto the streets of Northern Ireland at the beginning of the Troubles. By the time I had started primary school; I had experienced an arson attack on our home, the murder of an uncle and had been caught up in a booby trap blast bomb which claimed the life of a young British soldier.

Northern Ireland was a place of paradox, tragedy and bitter irony on a par with any Greek tragedy. By way of brief example - One uncle, a civil servant had been murdered by the UFF – a paramilitary grouping loyal to the British state; his brother, a policeman by the IRA, as he emerged from Sunday mass in the shadow of those very same dreary steeples.

By the time I had attended primary school we had moved to Derry/ Londonderry, as no-one can agree what it should be called - but that was the least of the city's many problems. At that point in the early 70s the city was still recovering from the events of Bloody Sunday which had witnessed the shooting of 26 unarmed civil rights protestors by paratroopers. Of those 26, some 14 in total were killed. The burning sense of injustice stemming decades culminated in the Saville Inquiry, which resulted in Prime Minister David Cameron stating in the House of Commons, that,

"... What happened on Bloody Sunday was both unjustified and unjustifiable. It was wrong.... on behalf of the government – and indeed our country – I am deeply sorry."

Peter Taylor OBE, a BBC investigative journalist, has reported on terrorism for 40 years. Smoking guns, like conspiracy theories, he recounts, are eagerly hunted by journalists but seldom found. They lie hidden locked in Government vaults but there is 'the odd glaring exception'. One such exception he cites from the Bloody Sunday inquiry, being the secret memorandum revealed by the Inquiry in which Major General Robert Ford warned, that to restore law and order, it would be necessary "to shoot selected ringleaders amongst the young hooligans after clear warnings had been issued".

As Lord Saville concluded in the Report on the Inquiries findings,

"What happened on Bloody Sunday strengthened the Provisional IRA,increased nationalist resentment and hostility towards the Army and exacerbated the violent conflict of the years that followed."

The most recent targeted killings in Yemen, Gaza and Pakistan by drone strikes is something I will return to later in the context of this lecture.

INTERNMENT WITHOUT TRIAL

The unprecedented campaign of violence in Northern Ireland resulted in the Government responding with a series of Measures including the Special Powers Act, which had been previously relied upon at times of crisis in NI. Under the legislation, any man could be interned without trial on 'suspicion of acting in any manner prejudicial to the preservation of peace and maintenance of order'.

Mr. Justice Maurice Gibson, who I return to later, ruled that access to legal representation and right of an internee to be informed of the suspicion against him - were to afforded in every instance – pretty fundamental rights, and the latter still topical today post Ward v PSNI, AF v Sec of State for the Home Dept., Al Rawi v The Security Service.

On 22nd January 2009 two days after his inauguration, a much younger looking, President Obama gave a speech at the US State Department in which he promised to close the facility at Guantanamo Bay – the lessons of this however were learned too late. The harshness of the regime during the Bush era did nothing to convey a healthy adherence to the rule of law. Somewhat akin to the controversy surrounding internment, it came all too late and only after a number of innocent people had been incarcerated.

To be falsely accused and hold a feeling of injustice was recently summed up by Lord McAlpine on how it felt to be wrongly implicated in a child sex abuse scandal when he said:

> "It gets into your bones ... it gets into your soul and you just think there's something wrong with the world."

The abolition of internment was replaced on foot of the recommendations by Lord Diplock in 1972. He concluded,

> "That until the current terrorism by the extremist organisations of both factions of Northern Ireland can be eradicated there will be some dangerous terrorists against whom it will not be possible to obtain convictions in any form of criminal trial which we regard as appropriate to a court of law..."

Bear in mind, 1972 saw the worst year of civil unrest in Northern Ireland – 10,628 shooting incidents, 1853 bombs or bombing incidents and 476 people killed. As a direct consequence a number of the controversial measures introduced included, non- jury, judge only courts, to deal with terrorist cases. It was undoubtedly one of the most significant departures from the Common Law.

This "temporary measure" remains in place and in operation forty years later - we still have non-jury 'Diplock' trials to deal with terrorist related offences. An article written in the Modern Law Review by a Professor of Law and Transitional Justice, at QUB, recently criticised lawyers for working this system in an article entitled *'What did Lawyers do during the 'War' ?'*

Well I make two observations about that:

(i) the Bar adapted accordingly in contesting trials before a judge alone, by way of its presentation of cases, encyclopedic and forensic knowledge of the rules of evidence, procedures and precedents to cope accordingly. The late Richard (Dick) Ferguson QC is an exemplar from that era.

(ii) The role of the Bar as a bulwark to injustice remains vital to a true and independent system of justice. Sir Sidney Kentridge QC spoke at the World bar Conference recently of his experiences, working at the Bar under apartheid. He recalled:

"now there were critics outside of South Africa & academic critics in particular, who said that we at the Bar in South Africa who appeared in the political cases against the govt., ought not to be doing that and the reason that they gave was that by appearing in these cases we were giving a veneer of respectability to what was actually a distorted, unfair & unjust system...

Well none of us I knew took any notice of that. We rather thought that it was the people at the sharp end, the accused in the criminal cases – in the terrorist cases – and so on , who had the first choice and oddly enough, no doubt because they were not as politically advanced as their critics, they on the whole preferred the chance of being acquitted rather than convicted. They preferred us to carry on....and carry on we most certainly did."

Sir Sidney - recently 90 years of age–deserves congratulations – is the epitome of what the Bar stands for and a true servant of the rule of law.

Other measures of expediency in NI included confession only convictions and supergrass trials...

THE USE OF CONFESSION EVIDENCE

In the days long before PACE, confessions made by an accused would be admissible evidence in cases involving paramilitary type offences, unless obtained by torture or inhuman or degrading treatment. By November 1977, the then Secretary of State for Northern Ireland, was informed by a number of solicitors, working in this field - including some referred to in the de Silva report, that

"Ill-treatment of suspects by police officers with the object of obtaining confessions, is now common practise."

One recent case of note is that of McCartney and McDermott, convicted on confession evidence of multiple offences of murder and membership of the IRA. Both spent several years in prison. Recently, our Court of Appeal quashed the convictions, declaring it felt a deep 'sense of unease' as to their safety. Raymond McCartney, is now the Vice-Chairman of the Justice Committee and a member of the devolved Stormont government.

One of the most controversial measures that came to the fore in the 1980's was ...

THE USE OF SUPERGRASS EVIDENCE

Some of the efforts deployed to curb terrorism in Northern Ireland during the Troubles must now be seen for the disasters they were. The use of the supergrass system is one such example. By the late 80s there was a marked decrease in the rates of successful convictions and by the late 80's the frailties of the system were easily exposed under the rigours of an adversarial system.

As the 80s wore on, Northern Ireland witnessed the IRA hunger strikes, the loyalist violence in the wake of the signing of the Anglo- Irish Agreement, and this year is the 25th anniversary of an IRA bomb exploding in Enniskillen at a remembrance day ceremony, not far from the same twin steeples of Fermanagh referred to by Churchill several decades before.

It was against this backdrop that barristers in Northern Ireland went about their daily business objectively, independently and professionally in the many trials, adhering to the cab rank rule, that invariably followed on from these and other similar events.

The year after the Enniskillen bombing I took up my place at law school. Not long after that, Northern Ireland witnessed the murder of prominent Belfast solicitor, Pat Finucane, less than four weeks after Douglas Hogg MP, during a Committee Stage debate on the Prevention of Terrorism (Temporary Provisions) Bill stated,

> "I have to state as a fact, but with great regret, that there are in Northern Ireland a number of solicitors who are unduly sympathetic to the cause of the IRA."

Allegations of state collusion in the murder continue and there have been several calls for an independent public inquiry from a number of bodies, including the US House of Representatives and Amnesty International compounded by the report produced by retired Canadian Supreme Court Justice, Peter Corey.

The report issued last week by Desmond de Silva QC, triggering an apology from David Cameron to the Finucane family, makes for chilling reading & I only touch upon his principal findings here –

As a result of his review Sir Desmond found,

i. that the threshold for a finding of collusion had been met;

ii. he was left in significant doubt as to whether Pat Finucane would have been murdered had it not been for the involvement of elements of the state;

iii. he was left in no doubt that agents of the State were involved in carrying out serious violations of human rights up to and including, murder, and in the aftermath of the Mr Finucane's murder there had been a "relentless attempt to defeat the ends of justice."

iv. Although he concluded there was no "over-arching" State conspiracy, he was unequivocal,

> "The abiding impression of this period in Northern Ireland must be of an extremely dark and violent time in which a lawyer could so callously and tragically be murdered as a result of discharging his professional legal duties."

It was against this backdrop that I began my career at the Bar in the early 90's...

The heavily fortified High Court, home of the High Court bench and Bar, had been bombed in the early 80s and had come under rocket attack in 1990's - with the never ending melody of the constant buzz of helicopters overhead.

Health and safety at work took on a whole new meaning....

During these years at the height of the Troubles, the Bar of Northern Ireland had a vital role to play in the administration of justice. Political views and sectarianism played no part in the role of the professionalism of a barrister in Northern Ireland... a robust, independent referral Bar and by extension an impartial and independent tribunal – to borrow the phraseology of Article 6 of the Convention - must be a sine qua non in any society facing such challenges.

It was during my early years at the Bar that I had been passed a bail application for a high profile republican that I first worked with the solicitor, Rosemary Nelson. Her client was one Colin Duffy, and she had gained notoriety when he previously had his conviction quashed in the Court of Appeal in Northern Ireland for the murder of a part time soldier, when post conviction , it had come to light that the key prosecution witness was later arrested in Scotland for gun running on behalf of loyalist paramilitaries.

Tragically, the same notoriety resulted in the murder of Rosemary a few years later...

Amongst cases in which she was involved was that of Sam Marshall. Marshall and two others, including Colin Duffy, were leaving the police station in Lurgan, Co. Armagh, having signed their bail – the details of attendance were known only to the police, the men and their solicitor. Shortly after leaving the station, within a few hundred yards of the police sangar, two men approached from a nearby vehicle and fired sixty eight shots, killing Sam Marshall - the two other men escaped. In a recent report from the Historical Enquiries Team, it seems the three men were under surveillance by the Security Service... up to moments before the shooting... the family maintain State collusion.

Some twenty years on, I recently appeared before the Coroner in Belfast - an inquest into this murder has now been scheduled – one of a number to arise by reason of several challenges brought to the European Court of Human Rights grounded upon the positive obligations of the State arising under article 2 of the Convention.

During the 1990's we saw Sinn Fein publicly entering talks with the British Government and Unionist parties. Gerry Adams, who once had charges of IRA membership quashed by Lowry J , who refused to allow 'speculation to take the place of inference' – now led his delegation into Castle Buildings, at Stormont.

In essence, this culminated in the power-sharing government which continues to operate today.

Mo Mowlam, the then Secretary of State aptly described it at the time, 'the peace we have now is imperfect, but better than none'.

Five days after, a huge bomb ripped through Co. Armagh, and a new breed of dissident republicanism emerged.

Despite this, the Good Friday Agreement was signed on 10th April 1998. The British and Irish Governments resolved their historical differences through the general and mutual acceptance of the principle of consent.

But the killings in Northern Ireland unfortunately did not end there and I shall return to that in due course but before I do, I wish to say something about the independence of our judiciary and the vital role they played during that time.

THE INDEPENDENCE OF THE JUDICIARY

At least 18 Republican attacks were carried out against the judiciary, resulting in the murders of two magistrates, two county court judges and Lord Justice Maurice Gibson who had ruled on the Special Powers Act, I mentioned earlier. One of those judges is the late Billy Doyle, an uncle of Brian Kennedy QC, my pupil master, here this evening.

One of core principles of the Rule of Law referred to by Raz is the independence of the judiciary which he felt 'must be guaranteed'. The judiciary in Northern Ireland is independent in every sense of the word – by the way, that includes jurisdictionally from the rest of the United Kingdom.

Presently in NI we still have Diplock trials, emergency legislation, and a judiciary and some members of the Bar who require personal protection officers at their side, accompanying them through their working day and beyond.

Our peace remains fragile as demonstrated in 2009 with the murder of two soldiers on the eve of their deployment to Afghanistan and more recently the murder of a prison officer on his way to work.

Arising out of both incidents I have appeared as part of the legal team for the one client in no less than three extended detention hearings under schedule 8 of the Terrorism Act relating to both incidents - debating the law on closed hearings, the power to grant bail, the right to disclosure, and the evidential basis of arrest.

In addition two judicial reviews before the Divisional Court concerning the compatibility sch 8 of the Terrorism Act and the Convention, (known as Duffy no1 & 2), a judicial review arising from the refusal by prison authorities to provide an assurance my consultation was not being covertly monitored (that's another story) and a six week non- jury trial for two counts of murder and 5 of attempted murders.

David Bentley BL & Paddy O'Connor QC from Doughty Street Chambers, who I know are here this evening, also appeared in that trial for the co- accused. In January this year, the trial judge Sir Anthony Hart returned 'not guilty' verdicts on each of the counts against the client for whom I had appeared together with Barry Macdonald QC, observing 'suspicion could not take the place of guilt'. I should add, that during that trial, Barry was also involved in a high profile loyalist trial and I was involved in the representation of a police officer. The cab rank rule lives strong.

Just last month, I found myself back in Antrim serious crime suite and after a hearing spanning late Saturday and all of Sunday, her Honour Judge Loughran declined an application by detectives for a further 7 day detention period, ordering the client's release having considered, inter alia, the principles enunciated in his previous cases of Duffy no.1 & no. 2 by the NI Divisional Court and also having considered AF & Ors before the Lords, and Al Rawi & Ors before the Supreme Court.

Demonstrative perhaps, that despite the pressures under which the judiciary in Northern Ireland continue to carry out their tasks and responsibilities in dispensing justice, they do so with an unyielding independence of mind that ensures that justice is done and seen to be done.

It is not just in N. Ireland however that the independence of the judiciary when dealing with terrorist cases has been demonstrated – we need only look back as far as the decision of Mr. Justice Mitting, in the most recent round of litigation between Secretary of State for the Home Department and Othman or Abu Qatada, as he is better known. David Blunkett, once described Abu Qatada as the 'most significant extremist preacher in the United Kingdom' and like Abu Hamsa, has become a hate figure in the popular press.

There was evidence at the first trial (where Abu Qatada was tried in absentia) from lawyers, medical examiners and relatives of the defendants who actually stood trial, showed visible signs of torture. One of these defendants, Abdul Nasser Al-Hamasher in his confession had stated that Abu Qatada had provided encouragement for the terrorist attacks. This was the principal evidence against Abu Qatada on that trial and Al-Hamasher maintained during his trial that his confession in which that evidence was contained had been procured by torture.

Now, as I understand, in Jordan the State does not have to prove that a statement made to a Public Prosecutor was made voluntarily. On the contrary, a defendant must not only prove that the confession was the result of oppression, he must also show that it was the consequence of illegal coercion to force him to confess to things which he had not done. The State Security Court in Jordan held that the defendant Al-Hamasher had failed to discharge that burden.

Abu Qatada was again tried in his absence in 2000. On this occasion the main evidence against him was again supplied by a co- defendant, this time one Abu Hawsher. During an appeal against his conviction, Abu Hawsher claimed to have been tortured during 50 days of interrogation and had in consequence made a confession to police. The Court of Cassation which heard his appeal dismissed this claim, finding it irrelevant because the State Security Court had not relied on it but had relied on a subsequent confession to the Public Prosecutor.

The legal, common, moral and political issues that Abu Qatada has provoked in Westminster must be viewed against the backdrop of the strict observance of the rule of law.

From the protracted jurisprudence I touch upon two of particular note in the context of this evening -

(a) At the initial stages of the deportation hearing upon appeal to the Court of Appeal, Buxton LJ, cited the ECtHR judgment of Jalloh v Germany 44 EHRR 32 which held that incriminating evidence-whether in the form of a confession or otherwise- obtained as a result of acts of violence, brutality or other forms of treatment which can be characterised as torture - should never be relied on as proof of the victim's guilt, irrespective of its probative value.

The court continued that any other conclusion would only serve to legitimise indirectly the sort of morally reprehensible conduct which the authors of Art.3 of the Convention sought to proscribe or, as it was put in the US Supreme Court's judgment in Rochin:

'to afford brutality the cloak of law'.

(b) At the subsequent proceedings post Lord Philips and the Lords, the Strasbourg court agreed with the observations of Lord Bingham in re A no. 2, - torture evidence is excluded because it is

> 'unreliable, unfair, offensive to ordinary standards of humanity and decency and incompatible with the principles which should animate a tribunal seeking to administer justice.'

The Court felt that 'experience has all too often shown that the victim of torture will say anything – true or not – as the shortest method of freeing himself from the torment of torture'. It continued

> "More fundamentally, no legal system based upon the rule of law can countenance the admission of evidence – however reliable – which has been obtained by such a barbaric practice as torture. The trial process is a cornerstone of the rule of law.
>
> Torture evidence damages irreparably that process; it substitutes force for the rule of law and taints the reputation of any court that admits it. Torture evidence is excluded to protect the integrity of the trial process and, ultimately, the rule of law itself."

I recently attended a symposium, aptly entitled 'The Supreme Court comes to Belfast' to hear Lords Kerr, Clarke, Dyson and Wilson, speak on a whole host of issues including that of Abu Qatada. Lord Kerr made the striking observation,

> "The Strasbourg court has made it clear that it and national courts should set their face against the admission of evidence produced by torture and that conclusion must resonate strongly with all who subscribe to the notion, that we should not require those who are entitled to look to the state for the protection of their fundamental rights, to accept a lesser standard of justice than we consider is the irreducible minimum of a fair trial".

It was against this backdrop that the decision of the Special Immigration Appeals Commission concluded that it had not been satisfied, despite whatever assurances had been obtained by the Secretary of State that there would be a fair trial.

The Sun Newspaper's headline read "Hate preacher Abu Qatada goes free as top judge sparks outrage".

I must remember to renew my subscription for 2013...

But it didn't stop with the press – some of whom called on the powers to be removed from the judiciary. Next came the politicians ...

First we heard from Nick Clegg, the Deputy Prime Minister ...

> "We strongly disagree with the court ruling, we're going to challenge it, we're going to take it to appeal. We're absolutely determined to see this man get on a plane and go back to Jordan."

Then it was the turn of David Cameron, the Prime Minister exhorting a similar view – 'we're all fed up' or words to that effect ... and finally, the recipient of the '2012 two fingers to the Rule of Law award' goes to the Right Honourable Peter Bone M.P. who addressed the Commons as follows,

> "You", (meaning Teresa May I assume)

> "You want to deport him, the Shadow Home Secretary wants to deport him, the Supreme Court says he can be deported, the British people say he should deported. Just deport him and worry about the consequences after".

Perhaps a word about ...

THE JUDICIARY AND THE GOVERNMENT

In the 1880s WS Gilbert suggested that when in the House of Commons, MPs had "to leave their brains outside and vote just as their leaders tell them to". Indeed, across the Irish Sea things were no different at times – the story is told of former Taoiseach Charles J Haughey, dining with the members of cabinet, when asked by the waiter, "and the vegetables, sir...?"

"They'll have what I'm having", came his reply.

The relationship between the judiciary and the Government was a theme touched upon by Lord Judge at the 16th Commonwealth conference in Hong Kong, when the issue then was one of Control Orders under the Prevention of Terrorism Act. Some may recall a former Home Secretary publicly criticise the "total refusal" of the Law Lords to discuss the issues of principle involved in these matters.

The former Home Secretary, felt it was time "for the senior judiciary to engage in a serious and considered debate about how best legally to confront terrorism in modern circumstances".

As the Irish comedian Jimmy Cricket would say, 'but wait there's more...' I defer to Lord Judge in the recouting,

> 'Accordingly he suggested that some "proper discussion" would be very helpful between the Law Lords and the Home Secretary, "in effect for the Law Lords to advise him about what steps might or might not be struck down".
>
> As Lord Judge observed
>
> "Such discussions would have represented one of those tiny first steps of which we should beware. When this issue was ventilated before the House of Lords Select Committee...the Committee considered it essential that the members of the court "should not even be perceived to have pre-judged an issue as a result of communications with the executive".

A blind man on a galloping horse could immediately see the potential for damage to public confidence in the independence of the judiciary – my thoughts, by the way, not those of Lord Judge!

McCloskey J speaking recently at the Bar Council conference in Belfast on 'Challenges to the Rule of Law in the 21st Century'– asked rhetorically,

"What does the rule of law require of all of us in the 21st century? The basic dogma is no different than before. The primary meaning of the rule of law is that everything must be done according to law...

Thus every Government Minister who, or Government agency which, purports to act in any given field must justify the action in question as authorised by law...

Acts of governmental power routinely affect the legal rights, duties and liberties of the individual. All such acts must be shown to have a strict legal pedigree.

The courts are the arbiters of whether the necessary legal pedigree exists".

With the Justice and Security Bill, back today before the Commons , having suffered a defeat last month in the Lords on the closed hearing material provisions - the Government may find its legal pedigree being tested in due course before the Courts, if it continues in it's current form.

The Sunday Times in a very telling editorial a few weeks back made the observation;

'If this Bill were to become an Act in its current form, those feeling that they had suffered a grave injustice at the hands of the Government would feel they had suffered another at the hands of the Courts'.

Lord Bingham's seminal treatise, springs to mind, when he outlined his core principle of the rule of law,

"That all persons and authorities within the state, whether public or private, should be bound by and entitled to the benefit of laws publicly made, taking effect in the future and publicly administered in the courts."

The rule of law and the independence, impartiality and transparency of the judiciary and judicial thinking are inseparable elements of a modern constitutional democracy. Plainly, the rule of law cannot function properly and effectively unless adjudication upon the legality of governmental acts is carried out by judges who are independent of the executive.

Raz, when speaking of judicial independence, the method of appointing Judges, the security of tenure, the way of fixing salaries and other conditions of service – is all designed to guarantee that the judiciary will be free from extraneous pressures and independent all of authorities save that of the law. They are, he concludes, essential for the preservation of the rule of law.

Judicial independence, is an internationally recognised value of longstanding. See, for example, the Resolutions of the General Assembly of the United Nations. In short, 'the independence of the judiciary derives from, and is an integral feature of, two seminal principles or doctrines: the first is the rule of law and the second is the separation of powers'.

Looking beyond these shores...

In the last number of weeks a presidential decree granting President Morsi, Egypt's Islamist leader, sweeping new powers was condemned by the country's top Judges as an unprecedented attack on the independence of the judiciary. The constitutional amendment issued by Morsi recently, granted him absolute power and immunity from judicial oversight until a new constitution is in place.

The decree insisted that the President's laws and decisions could not be challenged and many feel that the decree was a deliberate attempt to undermine Egypt's Judges, who have been at odds with the presidency since they dissolved the Muslim- brotherhood dominated parliament last June.

Just today the prosecutor general has submitted his resignation after 100's magistrates organised a sit in outside his office. I wonder has Michael Turner QC & the Criminal Bar been speaking to these guys??

In many ways the challenges facing our judiciary, the barracking from certain sections of the press and the, (at times) strained relationship with Parliament – has prompted the JAC to revise the job spec as follows..."Wanted Judge with integrity, independence and skin as thick as rhino hide".

This was taken up by Sir Sidney Kentridge QC:

> "... one aspect of the rule of law, on which we would certainly all agree, is the independence of the judiciary. It is secured, in part, by laws which give the judges security of tenure and in part by ensuring as far as possible that they are persons of integrity, appointed on merit rather than by reason of political connection ...
>
> There is a particular threat to judicial independence which should concern us. That is the growing tendency for politicians and the press to attack in intemperate and even vituperative terms judges

who have given decisions with which they disagree. Newspapers all too often respond to an unpopular decision with personal attacks on the judge concerned. Judges must accept strong criticism, even unfounded criticism …

One of the attributes we expect of an independent judge is the moral courage to make decisions which will be unpopular with politicians or the media or the public …"

Nevertheless the onslaught of criticism that does arise in contentious cases, must at times, be difficult to ignore, especially when headlines in the Daily Telegraph poll read, 'Should the Government Ignore the ruling and send Abu Qatada to Jordan' 93% of readers voted "Yes".

In many ways the same thick skin applies to posts judicial, foreign as well as domestic. I speak of course of...

THE ROLE OF THE EUROPEAN COURT OF HUMAN RIGHTS

In theearly daysoftheTroublestheIrish Government complained that a number of individuals persons had been subjected to torture, inhuman and degrading treatment and punishment within the meaning of Article 3 ECHR. In particular 5 interrogation techniques were complained of, including covering detainees' heads with hoods, sleep deprivation and loud noise.

The European Commission concluded that the 5 techniques amounted to 'torture and inhuman treatment' contrary to Article 3. The matter was thereafter referred to the ECtHR. The Court, in contrast to the Commission, held that the techniques did not amount to torture. However the Court still found that the techniques did amount to inhuman and degrading treatment in (see Ireland v United Kingdom 82 EHRR 25).

According to Professor Brice Dickson, of Queen's University Belfast, he states damage was done to the credibility of the Convention by this finding, falling short, by the Court on the question of what constituted 'torture'.

According to Dickson, unless the Court is bolder and less deferential than it has been to date regarding the protection of human rights during times of severe societal unrest, it will lose credibility as the foremost standard bearer for human rights in the world today.

With respect I don't agree & feel one need only look to thejurisprudence in recent times in particular relating to Northern Ireland for example the

Article 2, Article 5 & 6 cases & in recent weeks the MM case on article 8, successfully taken by the Bar pro bono committee - as well as the wealth of jurisprudence throughout the UK and beyond.

To cite Lord Kerr when speaking of the role of the Court in the domestic context:

> "...we need to get a better balance, a more mature perspective on our relationship with ECtHR and that we, as lawyers and judges, have our part to play in achieving that sense of steadi- ness. It is, I think, necessary to remind ourselves that the rela- tionship between national courts, particularly UK courts and the Strasbourg court is in its historical infancy."

He later opines in phraseology, no doubt acquired during his time at the Bar in Belfast,

> "If ever an institution deserves to be 'cut some slack', it is surely ECtHR. That is not to say that we should view its decisions with an uncritical eye but we need to be clear-sighted about what we can reasonably expect from such an institution."

[96] My own unswerving view is that the Strasbourg court has contributed massively to the raising of human rights standards in our country.

Turning to,

GLOBAL TERRORISM AND THE RULE OF LAW

The threat from global terrorism remains prevalent - to adopt the US phraseology 'enemies foreign and domestic' shall continue as long as there remains a US & UK presence outside of its own borders. The risks remain high and the methodology deployed in curbing the terrorist threat within the confines of the legal and moral maze are not always easy to reconcile.

President Elect Barrack Obama, prior to taking up office, received a detailed briefing from Mike McConnell, Director of National Intelligence.

It was only 2 days after his historical election in 2008 and he came away literally with the weight of the world on his shoulders – he made the observation -

"I'm inheriting a world that could blow up any minute in half a dozen ways, and I will have some powerful but limited and perhaps even dubious tools to keep it from happening."

The depth and fortitude of the global problem was disconcertingly reflected the following year by Khalid Sheikh Mohammed, the mastermind of 9/11.

"Your end is very near and your fall will be just as the fall of the towers on the blessed 9/11 day".

But the 'dubious tools' referred to by Obama, in many instances inherited from his predecessor, developed in the War on Terror' which has seen an increase in the use of covert action including drone strikes - initially authorised by President George Bush to target the Al Qaeda leadership in Pakistan. Fearing tip offs , Bush decided not to give prior notice to attacks upon individuals in another Sovereign State, his attitude typified when he said:

"OK, we're going to stop playing the game. These sons of bitches are killing Americans. I've had enough."

Perhaps no-one brought to his attention the comments of Supreme Court Justice Sandra Day O'Connor

"A state of war is not a blank cheque for the President."

Guantanamo Bay, was recently described by Lord Steyn on delivering the Clement Atlee memorial lecture , as 'a stain on American Justice '.

The Bush Administration's top secret memoranda authorising the CIA to carry out interrogation techniques on selected terrorist suspects show that abuse of those in detention was institutionalised. Their controversial release in 2010 was ordered by President Obama who wished to herald a new beginning by closing Guantanamo within a year of coming into office and bringing out into the open what the CIA had been authorised to do in America's name... yet drone strikes do continue and Guantanamo still remains open for business.

It is the view of at least some commentators, that the experience of being locked up in Guantanamo for years on end has only hardened the ideology of Al Qaeda. Many of the remaining detainees are regarded as the hard-core that no-one wants as well as high value detainees. Much like IRA and loyalist prisoners in the Maze, the detainees have a command structure and are organised on military lines, as, like the IRA, they see themselves as carrying on the fight in prison.

The shocking images of Abu Ghraib prison in Iraq shook the world. Donald Rumsfeld in his memoirs says he didn't know of the humiliations unfolding at the prison. The revelations of torture and abuse he said "left me feeling punched in the gut".

According to Professor Colin Campbell, elements in the US security apparatus have employed interrogation techniques in Iraq and in the wider war it bears striking resemblance to methods employed early on in Northern Ireland.

The investigative journalist Peter Taylor, writes:

> 'governments in the firing line justify their responses in the name of defending democracy and protecting the freedoms that Al Qaeda seeks to destroy, but in the process they handed the enemy incalculable propaganda opportunities'.

Taylor observed,

> "I watched these abuses in the decades since 9/11 as I had over 3 decades in Northern Ireland. Such are the dilemmas that Governments inevitably face in countering terrorism, as the British found in fighting in the IRA". He continued, "I reported on Bloody Sunday interment without trial and the abuse of detainees – all measures designed to crush the IRA – in fact had the opposite effect and only succeeded in creating more support for it."

The reality of terrorist atrocities and the ruthlessness of their perpetrators are sometimes lost in the propaganda war that is the offspring of violent conflict", Taylor forewarns.

Certainly the headlines in the weeks after 9/11 speak volumes... to quote one or two:

> "British to brief US on experience with IRA", (Daily Telegraph, 8th November 2001)
>
> and
>
> "Britain shares its lessons of terrorism", (Washington Times, 14th February 2002.)""

There are many lessons to be learned in the context of the International Rule of Law...

The role of the UK Government, both foreign and domestic, in dealing with the legal problems that arise in the course of fighting terrorism ,whether on the streets of Kabul, Belfast or Finsbury Park must be ever vigilant to the simple fact that as Raz points out, the deliberate disregard for the rule of law violates human dignity.

To look to a living, breathing example of this in our context we need look no further than the headlines in the Times last Friday;

'Britain to pay 2.2 million to family in Libya rendition'.

The Government has agreed to pay 2.2 million to the family of a 'Libyan dissident' who claimed that Jack Straw and MI6 played a part in their kidnap and forced return to Tripoli in 2004. Jack Straw is quoted as saying,

> "At all times I was scrupulous in carrying out my duties in accordance with the law."

The 'Libyan dissident', Sami al-Saadi, has been quoted as saying:

> "I started this process believing that a British trial would get to the truth. But today with the Government trying to push through secret courts, I feel that to proceed is not best for my family. I went through a secret trial once before in Gaddafi's Libya. In many ways , it was as bad as the torture. It is not an experience I care to repeat."

The 8th principle defining the rule of law, according to Raz, being the crime preventing agencies should not be allowed to pervert the law.

Taken in conjunction with the independence of the judiciary, it is designed to ensure that the legal machinery of enforcing the law, should not deprive it of its ability of supervising conformity to the rule of law and also provide effective remedies in cases of deviation from it.

Control orders, deportation orders, house arrests, extraditions, interrogation techniques, closed hearings and the increase in the prevalence of anti-terror legislation at every turn, all merit discussion in the context of the international rule of law...

It was US Supreme Court Justice Marshall who famously said in Skinner -v- Railway Labour Executives Association 489 US 602 1989:

> "History teaches us that grave threats to liberty often come in times of urgency, when constitutional rights seem too extravagant

to endure… when we allow fundamental freedoms to be sacrificed in the name of real or perceived exigency, we invariably come to regret it."

The question for any State to address, is that posed by Lord Neuberger …

"Q. how best to secure freedom through security, without security undermining freedom, but also without freedom undermining security?"

In an age of insecurity, in time of war or when the State faces a threat of domestic or international terror, this question as we know becomes all the more pressing.

The balance that has to be struck in maintaining the credibility and integrity of the Executive whilst ensuring the protection of all its citizens, is a high wire act. The war on terror may have many pluses however as the modern day face of terrorism is not so easy to identify or define, the delineation between black and white, friend or foe can be obscured in the mist of atrocity, tragedy and the need for retribution.

It is the judiciary and lawyers that play a vital role in all of this. Perhaps the words of John F Cash have a particular meaning for us all in the legal profession & justice system...

'I keep my eyes wide open all the time...because your mine, I walk the line.'

Strict observance of the separation of powers is an important guarantee in any democratic society to ensure the government also 'walk the line'. In a seminal Harvard Law Review article published after the attacks of September 11, 2001, President of Israeli Supreme Court, Barak J. defended a major role for judges in policing executive measures during times of crisis:

"Since its founding Israel has faced a security threat. As a Justice of the Israeli Supreme Court, how should I view my role in protecting human rights given this situation? I must take human rights seriously during times of both peace and conflict. I must not make do with the mistaken belief that, at the end of the conflict, I can turn back the clock".

Barak J. drew explicitly upon Lord Atkin's celebrated wartime dissent in Liversidge v Anderson [1942] A.C. 206 at 245 in which he championed the role of the judges in standing 'between the subject and any attempted encroachments on his liberty by the executive, alert to see that any coercive action is justified in law.'

Well what of the future... in terms of terrorism on a global perspective ?

In the last week, it was reported that growing numbers of young Saudis are joining the the fight against President Assad in Syria. Hugh Tomlinson, the Times reporter, observed former members of al-Qaeda, also leaving Saudi Arabia to join the fray. After a decade of struggling to bring the terrorist group to heel, there are fears in Riyadh that the mistakes of the past are being repeated, as the kingdom faces a fresh backlash from the battle-hardened jihadists when the fight for Damascus is won.'

Tomlinson observes, 'Al-Qaeda in Saudi Arabia is quietly back in circulation' or to put it in more colloquial terms closer to home ...

"They haven't gone away you know..."

We all hope that the lessons from the past help carve out rather than cloud our future in Northern Ireland & so - perhaps to end on a positive note ;

Those dreary steeples came back into view earlier this year when the Queen visited Enniskillen - Northern Ireland and the peace process has been steeped in symbolism for as along as the process has existed – the most recent scene recently played out - as she crossed the street from her service of thanksgiving at St. Macartans Protestant church to enter St. Michaels Roman catholic church – a first for a British Monarch - the crossing of the Rubicon from the past to the future.

The second came the next day with the handshake with the Queen and Martin McGuinness, a former IRA Commander.

Internment without trial, a supergrass system and the murders of lawyers are hopefully consigned to the past – in no short measure, due to the retention and maintenance of a truly independent referral Bar - an essential aspect of ensuring the rule of law is maintained. We have managed to do so by reason of our independence, our strict adherence to the cab rank rule and a collegiate library system that has served us well.

In no short measure the same can also be said of the judiciary, many of whom hail from the Bar. I feel we should have nothing but admiration for their unstinting dedication, commitment and professionalism, and above all, true independence that has ensured the embodiment of our system of justice.

Clearly in no short supply this side of the Irish sea as well...

At a time when the Bar has been under the cosh of swingeing cuts in the areas of publicly funded work, only ensures those who have represented their clients without fear or favour, are at risk of leaving the profession. By extension, the diversity of the pool of talent open to future generations of the judiciary shall be lost. The maintenance of the rule of law, I fear may suffer as a consequence in future years – that is perhaps, another talk for another day.

The central lesson if ever there is one when dealing with global terrorism, an international problem from a Northern Irish perspective, is this...

A democracy must defend itself from terrorism whilst striking the delicate balance between liberty and security – the rule of law denotes that fine line, that enunciates and underpins the necessity to uphold the principles central to our system of justice, which must remain true at all times, no matter how dark the day or even the hour.

The transition from conflict to conciliation, the world over, is made that much easier, in a system where the Rule of Law has been respected. The rule of law is a fundamental cornerstone in any democratic society and any turning of a blind eye, any breaking of the rules or digression from the core values, comes at a cost that can take generations to overcome...

Openness and the Rule of Law

THE RIGHT HONOURABLE BEVERLEY MCLACHLIN, P.C.

Chief Justice of Canada

8 January 2014

I. INTRODUCTION

It is a great honour to have been asked to present the Annual International Rule of Law Lecture. The honour is only deepened by the association between this lecture and the late Lord Bingham, whose memory we revere. No one did more to promote the rule of law throughout the world than Tom Bingham, whose book is rightly seen as the bible on the subject.

Today, I take as my theme one of the elements of the rule of law Lord Bingham set out in his book – the principle of open justice. Lord Bingham held that the core of the rule of law is the principle "that all persons and authorities within the state, whether public or private, should be bound by and entitled to the benefit of laws publicly made, taking effect (generally) in the future and *publicly administered in the courts*."[1]

The open court principle is a venerable principle, deeply rooted in western consciousness. And for good reason. As Jeremy Bentham famously put it:

> Where there is no publicity there is no justice. Publicity is the very soul of justice. It is the keenest spur to exertion and the surest of all guards against improbity. It keeps the judge himself while trying under trial.[2]

Or as Justice Brandeis succinctly expressed it, "Sunshine is said to be one of the best disinfectants."[3]

[1] Tom Bingham, *The Rule of Law* (London: Penguin Group Ltd., 2010) at 8.

[2] Quoted in *A.G. (Nova Scotia) v. MacIntrye*, [1982] 1 S.C.R. 175 at 183, *per* Dickson J. (as he then was).

[3] "What Publicity Can Do", *Harpers Weekly* (December 20, 1913).

We insist on open justice so that citizens may know how justice is being rendered. Courts must be open and reasons for judgment public so that the litigants, the media, legal scholars and ultimately the general public may follow, scrutinize and criticize what is done in the name of justice. It is a point of pride that long before transparency became the buzzword of governance, the courts insisted that their proceedings be open to all.

Yet open justice, important as it is, comes at a cost. It exists in tension with two other things that we value – privacy and security. In Bentham's time, the tension between open courts on one hand, and privacy and security on the other, was minimal and hence seldom discussed. In our time, the tension has increased exponentially as a consequence of an increased emphasis on privacy, technology, and national security. The result is that the open court principle – and with it the rule of law – stands in peril as never before. This begs the question: is the open court principle sustainable in the 21st century?

To answer this question, I wish to explore with you what has changed and what we can do about it. I will suggest that much as we might wish to, we can no longer think of open justice as an absolute principle, before which all other considerations must fall. Instead, the courts must balance the open justice principle against countervailing interests of privacy and security. The question in each case is where and how to draw the line.

This is not an easy task. Judges, guided by counsel, must identify the values at stake in a particular case and consider how they are likely to play out. The goal is to draw the line at the point where privacy and security are appropriately protected, yet the essentials of the open justice principle are maintained. The science is not exact, to be sure. Yet the task can be accomplished if the judge identifies and carefully evaluates what is at stake on both sides of the issue. It is all too easy in this arena to allow emotion and fear to cloud judgment, skewing the balance in favour of privacy or security. The antidote is reasoned identification and examination of what is really at stake in the case at hand. In this way, we can sustain the fundamental principle of open justice, while also responding to changing circumstances and priorities.

II. THE TRADITIONAL OPEN COURT PRINCIPLE

We must first ask ourselves: what is the open court principle?

The open court principle can be reduced to two fundamental propositions. First, court proceedings, including the evidence and documents tendered, are open to the public. Second, juries give their verdicts and judges deliver their judgments in public or in published form.

It is also important to note what the common law open court principle *is not*. It does not require all aspects of the judicial process be open to the public. For example, a judge's private deliberations remain private and evidence may be protected by privileges, such as informer's privilege, that allow some facts to remain private.

The next question is: why is open justice so important?

Open justice serves three important functions: (1) it assists in the search for truth and plays an important role in educating the public by permitting access to and dissemination of accurate information;[4] (2) it ensures and enhances judicial accountability, deterring misconduct by judges, police officers and prosecutors; and (3) it performs a therapeutic function by permitting the community to see that justice is done.[5] In these ways, the open courts principle works to preserve public confidence in the administration of justice, which is essential to the rule of law.

The principle of open justice is not new. The idea that judicial proceedings should be public is as old as the trial itself. Before the Norman Conquest, trials were being held in the mandatory presence of the freemen of the local community, who were called upon to render judgment.[6]

Over time, this system evolved so that only a representative body of freemen was required to attend hearings and pass judgment on behalf of the community. The modern jury system was born. Although the public's attendance at trials was no longer required, trials remained open and the importance of public attendance was recognized.[7] Gradually, the tradition of open justice became enshrined as a central tenet of the English justice system,[8] and spread throughout the western world and beyond.

Thus in 1892, Canada's first *Criminal Code* endorsed the common law principle that every court "shall be deemed an open and public court, to

[4] See S.E. Harding, "Cameras and the Need for Unrestricted Electronic Media Access to Federal Courtrooms", (1995-1996) 69 S. Cal. L. Rev. 827, at 845.

[5] See *Richmond Newspapers, Inc. v. Virginia*, 448 U.S. 555 (1980).

[6] Jack B. Harrison, "How Open is Open – the Development of the Public Access Doctrine under State Open Court Provisions" (1991-1992) 60 U. Cin. L. Rev. 1307 at 1308-1309; see also: *Richmond Newspapers, supra*, at 565.

[7] *Ibid.*

[8] *Ibid.*

which the public may generally have access so far as the same [room] can conveniently contain them".[9]

Until recently, this fundamental principle was viewed as virtually absolute, subject only to certain exceptions. In a few narrowly circumscribed situations, the privacy interests of litigants and witnesses were allowed to trump the open court principle – where this was essential to a fair criminal trial, in litigation involving wards, in lunacy proceedings, and in disputes over trade secrets.[10] In all other cases, the open court principle was held to be paramount.

In 1913, the House of Lords in *Scott v. Scott* opined that while public hearings may be trying for parties and witnesses, this is tolerated and endured because openness is the best means for establishing public confidence and respect in the administration of justice.[11]Lord Atkinson acknowledged that the hearing of a case in public may be "painful, humiliating, or deterrent both to parties and witnesses" and in some cases, "the details may be so indecent as to tend to injure public morals".[12] Nonetheless, the open courts principle prevails. Lord Shaw acknowledged that the fear of giving evidence in public may deter witnesses from giving testimony, but concluded that "the concession to these feelings would ... tend to bring about those very dangers to liberty in general, and to society at large, against which publicity tends to keep us secure..."[13]

Across the Atlantic, the Supreme Court of Canada, affirmed the importance of the open court principle in 1982, stating:

> It is now well established, however, that covertness is the exception and openness the rule. Public confidence in the integrity of the court system and understanding of the administration of justice are thereby fostered. As a general rule the sensibilities of the individuals involved are no basis for exclusion of the public from judicial proceedings.[14]

With the advent of the *Canadian Charter of Rights and Freedoms*, the open court principle was recognized as a component of freedom of expression,

[9] Jamie Cameron, "Victim Privacy and the Open Court Principle" (2003) Department of Justice Canada at 7.

[10] *Scott v. Scott*, [1913] A.C. 417 at 482 (House of Lords).

[11] *Ibid* at 463.

[12] *Ibid*.

[13] *Ibid* at 485.

[14] *Nova Scotia (Attorney General) v. MacIntyre*, [1982] 1 S.C.R. 175 at 185, *per* Dickson J. for the majority.

protected by s. 2(b) of our *Charter*.[15] This meant that the government was foreclosed from legislating closed hearings or publication bans unless the limit on freedom of expression was "demonstrably justified in a free and democratic society" under s. 1 of our *Charter*.

In short, court proceedings have historically been open, unless the case fell within a few recognized exceptional categories. Open justice was generally presumed to trump other interests. As we shall presently see, that presumption has been challenged in recent years as the growing importance of other interests has been recognized.

III. THE PRIVACY PRINCIPLE

The first challenge to the open court principle in the 21st century has been an increasing emphasis on privacy rights.

The right to privacy is the handmaid to several interests worth protecting. It is, in the words of Professor Daniel Solove, a "pluralistic value". It protects:

> intimacy, friendship, dignity, individuality, human relationships, autonomy, freedom, self-development, creativity, independence, imagination, counterculture, eccentricity, freedom of thought, democracy, reputation, and psychological well-being.[16]

As George Orwell saw so clearly in his dystopian novel *1984*, the modern panoptic state has the potential to undermine these values are so essential to human flourishing. In 2013, however, the dangers are posed not only by the state, but insidiously by private enterprise's efforts to amass our personal details so that they can more effectively target us as consumers of their products. By some estimates, there is more personal information – about our tastes, religious and political beliefs, sexual proclivities, and reading and viewing habits – in the hands of corporations than in the hands of any one state.

Traditionally, as *Scott v. Scott* attests, privacy did not count for much in court. Apart from a few exceptions, the public could attend any court hearing, consult any court document, and examine any judgment – regardless of what intimate or embarrassing details of litigants' and

[15] *Edmonton Journal v. Alberta (Attorney General)*, [1989] 2 S.C.R. 1326

[16] Daniel J. Solove, *Understanding Privacy* (Cambridge: Harvard University Press, 2008) at 98.

witnesses' lives may be revealed. Indeed, one searches the old common law cases in vain for an articulated principle of privacy. Perhaps one of the earliest statements of a privacy right is found in the celebrated *Seyman's Case*,[17] which provides that a man is secure from unreasonable search and seizure within his own home. Summing up the principle, Sir Edward Coke famously proclaimed that "[t]hat the house of every one is to him as his Castle and Fortress as well for defence against injury and violence, as for his repose".[18] The privacy interest in this statement is implicit. It is cloaked in the language of property rights and the notion of sanctuary – in the principle that "everyone's house is his safest refuge"[19] – rather than an articulated principle of privacy.

Two seemingly contradictory developments have challenged this anemic conception of privacy in more modern times.

The first was the articulation of privacy as a right or legal entitlement.

In their seminal article, *The Right to Privacy*, Samuel Warren and Louis Brandeis discussed the importance of protecting one's private life in the age of modern media and advocated for a right to privacy under the law.[20] They wrote:

> Instantaneous photographs and newspaper enterprise have invaded the sacred precincts of private and domestic life; and numerous mechanical devices threaten to make good the prediction that "what is whispered in the closet shall be proclaimed from the house-tops." For years there has been a feeling that the law must afford some remedy for the unauthorized circulation of portraits of private persons…

In 1965, the United States Supreme Court recognized a constitutional right to privacy in affirming the right to use contraception. It stated that the various constitutional provisions created "zones of privacy" into which the state could not intrude.[21] Eight years later, the U.S. Supreme Court affirmed the constitutional right to privacy in *Roe v. Wade*.[22] The right to privacy entered the jurisprudential lexicon.

[17] (1604) Michaelmas Term, 2 James 1 In the Court of King's Bench.
[18] The *Reports*, volume 5, page 91a.
[19] *Domus sua cuique est tutissimum refugium.*
[20] Samuel Warren and Louis Bradeis, "The Right to Privacy" (1890) 4 Harv. L. Rev. 193.
[21] *Griswold et al. v. Connecticut*, 381 U.S. 479 (1965).
[22] 410 U.S. 113 (1973).

The idea spread. In 1982, Canada adopted a constitutionally entrenched *Charter of Rights and Freedoms.* Section 7 guaranteed the right to "life, liberty and security of person", which the courts construed as including privacy rights. Section 8 protects individuals from unreasonable search or seizure, and implicitly creates a zone of privacy into which the state cannot unreasonably intrude.[23] The right to privacy is also explicitly protected by articles 3 and 35-7 of the *Civil Code* of Quebec.[24]

The Ontario Court of Appeal recently concluded that invasion of privacy constitutes an actionable tort, provided : 1) the defendant's conduct was intentional; 2) the defendant invaded, without lawful justification, the plaintiff's private affairs or concerns; and 3) a reasonable person would regard the invasion as highly offensive causing distress, humiliation, or anguish.[25] The rationales for affirming a tort of privacy included the importance of the value of privacy, the constitutional dimension of privacy, and technological changes that pose novel threats to the right of privacy.[26]

Most U.S. states have also recognized a tort of invasion of privacy.[27] Four Canadian provinces have statutorily created that tort.[28]

The criminal law has also moved to increase privacy protection for victims, complainants and children. For example, in Canada, we have come to recognize the importance of protecting the privacy of victims of sexual abuse.[29] The concern is that complainants may be further victimized by the violation of their privacy and, more broadly, that the administration of justice may be harmed if complainants refuse to pursue complaints because of privacy concerns.[30]

Many jurisdictions, including Canada, have enacted limits on the open court principle to protect the privacy rights of children. Section 110 of the *Youth Criminal Justice Act*,[31] prohibits publication of information that may identify the young accused, and s. 111 prohibits the publication of any

[23] *Hunter v. Southam Inc.*, [1984] 2 S.C.R. 145; *R. v. Dyment*, [1988] 2 S.C.R. 417; *R. v. Mills*, [1999] 3 S.C.R. 662.
[24] S.Q. 1991, c. 64.
[25] *Jones v. Tsige*, 2012 ONCA 32, 108 O.R. (3d) 241 at para. 71.
[26] *Ibid* at paras. 66 – 69.
[27] *Ibid* at para. 55.
[28] *Privacy Act*, R.S.B.C. 1996, c. 373 (British Columbia); *Privacy Act*, R.S.M 1987, c. P125 (Manitoba); *Privacy Act*, R.S.S. 1978, c. P-24 (Saskatchewan); *Privacy Act*, R.S.N.L., 1990, c. P-22.
[29] *Criminal Code*, s. 486.4.
[30] *Canadian Newspapers Co. v. Canada (Attorney General)*, [1988] 2 S.C.R. 122.
[31] S.C. 2002, c. 1.

information that may identify a young victim or witness in connection with an offence committed by a youth.

Provincial child protection legislation often provides for closed hearings and publication bans. For example, under the Ontario *Child and Family Services Act*,[32] child protection hearings are heard in private, unless the court orders otherwise. Certain media representatives may be present, but the court has the discretion to exclude the media or prohibit publication if it would cause emotional harm to the child.

Finally, in direct conflict with the open court principle, s. 486 of the Canadian *Criminal Code* provides that a judge may exclude all or any members of the public from the court room if it is in the "interests of public morals, the maintenance of order or the proper administration of justice…" In *Canadian Broadcasting Corp. v. New Brunswick (Attorney General)*,[33] the Supreme Court of Canada considered the constitutional validity of this limitation on the open court principle and concluded that while it violates freedom of expression, it is justified. It preserves the general principle of openness in most situations, but also gives the court a way to protect the privacy interests of innocent victims in appropriate cases. The Court held that s. 486 "arms the judiciary with a useful and flexible interpretive tool to accomplish its goal of preserving the openness principle, subject to what is required by the administration of justice…"[34]

In England, privacy has entered legal doctrine via Article 8 of the Convention for the Protection of Human Rights and Fundamental Freedoms, 4 November 1950,[35] incorporated by the *Human Rights Act* 1998 (U.K.).[36] The House of Lords has declined to recognize a common law tort of invasion of privacy.[37] However, the tort of breach of confidence captures the misuse of private information.[38] As in Canada, various criminal and civil statutes impose restrictions on the open court principle in the name of privacy. And as in Canada, the U.K. has passed laws protecting the identity of victims of sexual offences and children involved in the criminal justice system.[39]

32 R.S.O. 1990, c. 11.
33 [1996] 3 S.C.R. 480.
34 *Ibid* at para. 60.
35 213 U.N.T.S. 221
36 1998 c. 42.
37 *Wainwright v. Home Office*, [2003] UKHL 53, [2003] 4 All E.R. 969.
38 *Campbell v. MGN Ltd.*, [2004] UKHL 22, [2004] 2 A.C. 457.
39 Cameron, *supra*, at 43-44.

The tension between the open court principle and the competing principle of privacy is evident in the recent debates about the U.K. Family Courts. Public access to hearings on family matters is highly restricted. Most family proceedings are heard in private, and while duly accredited members of the media are entitled to attend private hearings, the court retains the power to exclude them and reporting is limited. In most cases, the media representatives are not entitled to receive or examine court documents.[40] And few judgments are made available to the public.[41]

Many have called for increases in the openness and transparency of the Family Courts. Recently, Sir James Munby, the president of the Family Division, issued a draft practice guidance calling for greater transparency to improve public understanding of court processes and confidence in the court system. In particular, he suggests presumptions in favour of publishing judgments.[42]

Overall, the trend appears clear. The open court principle continues to be a fundamental part of our society, but more and more privacy concerns are limiting it. The increasing protection of privacy interests in manifest forms and guises is increasingly circumscribing the open court principle.

Yet this is not the whole story. A second and countervailing development has been simultaneously undermining of the right to privacy. I speak of technological advances in communications. Paradoxically, while courts and legislators have been advancing privacy interests, technology has been working to destroy them. The digital revolution put smart phones and Facebook into the hands of millions. People voluntarily revealed -- and continue to reveal -- immense quantities of private information pertaining not only to themselves but to others within their particular cyberspace. What they choose not to reveal can be obtained by the state, as Edward Snowden's leaks have revealed. And overarching all this is the information that Google has placed in the ubiquitous "Cloud". As one Silicon Valley boss reportedly remarked, "Privacy is dead. Get over it."[43] Or as Mark Zukerberg, the founder of Facebook, put it, privacy is no longer a "social norm".[44]

[40] Adam Wolanski and Kate Wilson, "The Family Courts: Media Access and Reporting"(2011), a joint publication of the President of the Family Division, the Judicial College, and the Society of Editors.

[41] *Ibid.*

[42] Draft Practice Guidance issued by Sir James Munby, "Transparency in the Family Courts and the Court of Protection" (12 July 2013).

[43] Timothy Garton Ash, *Globe and Mail*, "Government Spying? Worry About Yourself", November 1, 2013, p. A15.

[44] *The Economist*, "The people's panopticon", November 16, 2013, p. 29.

This second trend – the negative impact of technology on privacy – also conflicts with the open court principle. In Bentham's day, technical barriers to the mass collection and distribution of information offered some protection to the privacy of participants in the justice system. Only those who were able to attend the court or read newspapers followed court proceedings. Today, television, the internet, and social media provide for the immediate dissemination of information to a vast audience. In the era of 21st century technology, the open court principle can mean an enormous loss of privacy.[45] In short, the paradigm shift in communication that we are living through has necessitated a change in how we apply the open court principle.

Consider the following. In the United States, Canada and other jurisdictions, electronic filing of court documents, including affidavits, is routine. Following the open court principle, a number of jurisdictions in the United States moved to allow public access to these documents. At the touch of a key, personal details of the parties' conduct, alleged conduct and finances were immediately accessible to anyone who cared to log on. When people had to go to the courthouse and ask for a file, few accessed such information. When it was simply a matter of striking a few keys in the privacy of one's home, thousands did.[46]

The same paradigm shift may give rise to claims for the protection of the anonymity of litigants to counter the reality of mass distribution. A recent case in the Supreme Court of Canada, *A.B. v. Bragg Communications Inc.*,[47] concerned a 15 year old girl victimized by a fake, highly sexualized Facebook page. Her father sued the internet provider to obtain information identifying the offender, with a view to suing him for defamation. Normally, parties to litigation must declare who they are. However, in this case, the father asked for an order banning the publication of the girl's identity and the details of the Facebook page, on the ground that publication of these would further injure his daughter. The lower courts denied the publication bans. Reversing those decisions, the Supreme Court emphasized the inherent vulnerability of children, the harms to children as a result of cyber-bullying, and the harms to the administration of justice if children decline to take steps to protect themselves because of the risk of further harm from public disclosure. These harms outweighed the open

45 Chief Justice Beverly McLachlin, "Courts, Transparency, and Public Confidence – To the Better Administration of Justice" (2003) 8 Deakin L. Rev. 1 at 3.

46 Karen Eltis, "The Judicial System in the Digital Age: Revisiting the Relationship between Privacy and Accessibility in the Cyber Context" (2011) 56:2 McGill L.J. 289.

47 2012 SCC 46, [2012] 2 S.C.R. 567.

court principle, warranting a publication ban. This said, the Court confined the publication ban to information that would identify the complainant; the public's right to open courts and press freedom prevailed with respect to the non-identifying Facebook content. The order was justified, the Court said, because the internet allows cyber- bullies to follow children wherever they go and to spread information widely, quickly, and anonymously.[48]

One thing seems clear. In an age of immediate access to vast amounts of information, it is becoming ever more difficult to reconcile concerns for the privacy, reputation and well-being of individuals engaged in the justice system with the principle of the open and public administration of justice.[49] We all agree that the open court principle is critical to maintaining public confidence in the judiciary, and in turn, fostering the rule of law. However, we must face the question: given the tugs of increasing insistence on privacy on the one hand, and the impact of technology on the dissemination of private data on the other, how will we sustain the open court principle in today's society?

The regulation of the media's access to and publication of litigants' personal information can take different forms. Courts can and ought to continue their case-by-case supervision through confidentiality orders and publication bans. Ultimately, it is the responsibility of the courts to balance the open court principle against the right to privacy. But other forms of regulation of the dissemination of litigants' data can be a useful auxiliary to the courts' direct supervision. At one end of the spectrum, the press can self-regulate through codes of conduct and industry complaint bodies. Information and privacy commissioners can play a role by issuing guidance in relation to the obtaining and use by the press of litigants' personal data. This kind of "soft" law can have a salutary effect, even if it does not have binding force. And at the other end of the spectrum, the law could regulate the media's activities through data-protection legislation.

2. National Security

The second concern increasingly impinging on the open court principle is national security. "Our fidelity to the open court principle was nurtured in a stable democracy, in peaceful times."[50] Now the open court principle must adapt to unstable times and the global threat of terrorism. Since the September 11, 2001, attacks on the World Trade Center Towers, national

48 *Ibid* at para. 22.

49 Chief Justice McLachlin, *supra*, at 4.

50 D.M. Paciocco, "When Open Courts Meet Closed Government" (2005) 29 S.C.L.R.(2d) 385 at 386-7.

security has become a priority for many governments, and there is a heightened need to keep sources and intelligence secret.[51] The state's highest duty is to protect its citizens, it is argued. In a world where the disclosure of information can endanger populations and jeopardize national security efforts, the transnational threat of terrorism makes sharing intelligence between states essential. Cooperation and coordination are in turn premised on mutual commitments that the shared information will be kept confidential.[52] The result has been ever-greater limits on the openness of judicial proceedings that involve national security issues. The person charged or threatened with deportation may be denied access to the information used against him. And the public and the press are left unable to judge whether the court proceedings are fair and the result just.

Countries across the globe have passed laws limiting access to national security evidence and information in court proceedings. In Canada, anti-terrorism legislation enacted after 9/11 provided for increased discretionary and mandatory publication bans and secret hearings to prevent injury to international relations or national security.[53] This has limited public and press access to judicial proceedings.

Not surprisingly, many of these legislative provisions have been challenged as an unreasonable limit on freedom of expression. Canadian courts were asked to strike a balance between the principle of openness, enshrined in our *Charter*, and national security concerns in a post 9/11 world.

In *Ruby v. Canada (Solicitor General),*[54] the Supreme Court of Canada heard a constitutional challenge to a provision in the *Privacy Act*[55] that provided for mandatory *in camera* and *ex parte* judicial review proceedings where a request for personal information was denied on national security grounds. The Court reiterated the importance of the open court principle, but also recognized that national security is a pressing and substantial concern and closed hearings reduce the risk of an inadvertent disclosure of sensitive information. Balancing these competing imperatives, the Court concluded that the requirement that the entire judicial review proceeding be heard *in camera* was an unreasonable limit on freedom of expression.

51 *Ibid* at 387.

52 David Cole, Federico Fabbrini and Arianna Vedaschi, *Secrecy, National Security, and the Vindication of Constitutional Law*, (United Kingdom: Edward Elgar Publishing Ltd., 2013) at 2.

53 *Anti-Terrorism Act*, S.C. 2001, c. 41. See also: Pacciocco, *supra*.

54 2002 SCC 75, [2002] 4 S.C.R. 3.

55 R.S.C. 1985, c. P-21.

The Court was again asked to determine the appropriate balance between openness and national security interests in *Re Vancouver Sun*.[56] Canadian anti-terrorism legislation created a new procedure for investigative hearings, allowing investigators to compel potential witnesses to provide information during terrorism investigations. In this case, the government obtained an order that the hearing was to be held *in camera* and no notice was to be given to the accused, the press, or the public. Subsequently, the witness challenged the constitutional validity of the investigative hearing procedure. The hearing on the constitutional issue was held *in camera* and the reasons for judgment were sealed. The Court criticized the level of secrecy in this case, noting that the facts of this case illustrate "how antithetical to the judicial process secret court hearings are."[57] The Court concluded that the constitutional hearing should have been held in open court and the judicial investigative hearing was to be held in public. This case represents a strong affirmation of the open court principle, even in the context of national security. Indeed, the Supreme Court of Canada heard the appeal from the constitutional challenge entirely in open court, subject to some restrictions.[58]

More recently, the Supreme Court of Canada held that the security certificate regime in Canadian immigration law was unconstitutional.[59] This regime permitted the government to issue security certificates, leading to the detention and ultimate deportation of a non-citizen deemed to be a threat to national security. The certificate and detention were subject to review by a judge, but upon the government's request, the review was conducted *in camera* and *ex parte*. The named person had no right to see the material upon which the case against him was based.[60] The Court found this procedure unconstitutional because it resulted in the detainee being denied full information about the case against him.

Last autumn, the Supreme Court of Canada heard yet another constitutional challenge to the revised security certificate regime.[61] Under the legislation, we were obliged to hold part of our hearing *in camera* at a secret location. Much of the evidence and part of the judgments on review were secret.

[56] 2004 SCC 43, [2004] 2 S.C.R. 332.
[57] *Ibid* at para. 52.
[58] *Ibid* at para. 20.
[59] *Charkaoui v. Canada (Citizenship and Immigration)*, 2007 SCC 9, [2007] 1 S.C.R. 350.
[60] *Ibid* at paras. 4-9.
[61] *Ministry of Citizenship and Immigration, et al. v. Mohamed Harkat, et al.* (34884).

The challenge of balancing openness against national security concerns is increasingly confronting Canadian judges. For example, the Federal Court has considered provisions requiring closed hearings when determining whether national security information should be disclosed.[62] The Court held that these provisions were an unjustified limit on the open court principle – but only to the extent that they apply when there is no secret information being reviewed by the court and the court sessions and court records are available to all parties. The provisions remain valid when secret information is in play.[63]

In the United States, shortly after the terrorist attacks of 9/11, the Chief Immigration Judge issued a directive to all United States Immigration Judges requiring a closure of "special interest cases", including certain deportation cases. The issue before the U.S. Court of Appeals for the Sixth Circuit was whether this violated the First Amendment.[64] Strongly affirming the open court principle, the court stated:

> Democracies die behind closed doors. The First Amendment, through a free press, protects the people's right to know that their government acts fairly, lawfully, and accurately in deportation proceedings. When government begins closing doors, it selectively controls information rightfully belonging to the people. Selective information is misinformation. The Framers of the First Amendment "did not trust any government to separate the true from the false for us"… They protected the people against secret government.[65]

The court added that "open proceedings, with a vigorous and scrutinizing press, serve to ensure the durability of our democracy"[66] concluding that the press and public have a First Amendment right of access to deportation hearings. Yet we are told that electronic eavesdropping by the federal government is monitored by the Foreign Intelligence Surveillance Court, a court consisting of a panel of selected judges, sitting in secret.[67]

The competing principles of openness and national security are also at play in the recent debates and discussion surrounding closed material proceedings in the U.K. CMP's were first introduced in the late 1990's to facilitate the hearing of deportation cases that raised national security

62 *Toronto Star v. Canada*, 2007 F.C. 128.
63 *Ibid* at para. 2.
64 *Detroit Free Press, et al. v. John Ashcroft, et al.*, 303 F.3d 681 (3d Cir. 2002).
65 *Ibid* at 683.
66 *Ibid* at 711.
67 "In Secret, Court Vastly Broadens Powers of N.S.A.", New York Times, July 6, 2013.

issues. At that time, they were exceptional.[68] Under a CMP, the court sits in private and sensitive information is only disclosed to the court and Special Advocates appointed by the government to represent the other party's interests. The other party does not see the sensitive evidence.[69] In the past decade, the U.K. Parliament introduced legislation allowing for CMP's in certain terrorism cases.[70]

In *Al Rawi v. Security Service*,[71] the claimants brought proceedings against the Security Services for damages arising from the government's complicity in their detention and ill treatment by foreign authorities. The government claimed that the material for its defence was sensitive and requested that part of the hearing proceed by way of a CMP. The issue before the Court was whether it had the power to order a CMP for the whole or part of a civil trial for damages. The Court affirmed the important principle of open justice, but also recognized the growing need to balance that principle against national security interests. Ultimately, the Court concluded that CMP's are such a significant departure from the common law principles of openness and natural justice, that only Parliament can bring about such a fundamental change.

In *Bank Mellat v. HM Treasury*,[72] the Supreme Court considered whether it could conduct a closed hearing when the statute in question provided for CMP's in the lower courts. In concluding that it could adopt a CMP under the *Counter-Terrorism Act 2008*, the Court reiterated the open court principle,[73] but held that CMP's may be necessary to promote the *Act*'s aim of protecting the country from threats of terrorism.[74]

The use of CMP's in the U.K. has expanded with the enactment of the *Justice and Security Act*.[75] Enacted this past year, the *Act* expands the use of "closed material proceedings" in civil cases.

When the *Justice and Security Bill* was first introduced, there was much debate about whether it struck the appropriate balance between transparency in court proceedings and the secrecy that national security

[68] Lord Justice Stephen Sedley, "Terrorism and Security: Back to the Future?" in David Cole, Federico Fabbrini and Arianna Vedaschi, eds., *Secrecy, National Security, and the Vindication of Constitutional Law* (United Kingdom: Edward Elgar Publishing Ltd., 2013) 13 at 21.
[69] *Al Rawi v. Security Service*, [2011] UKSC 34 at para. 2.
[70] *Ibid* at para. 27.
[71] *Al Rawi, supra.*
[72] [2013] UKSC 38.
[73] *Ibid* at para. 2.
[74] *Ibid* at paras. 51-54.
[75] 2013, c. 18.

sometimes demands. The House of Lords expressed concerns that CMP's offend the principle of open justice, saying:

> A CMP is inherently damaging to the integrity of the judicial process. Judicial decisions are respected precisely because all the evidence is heard in open court and can be reported, subject to exceptions, and judges give a reasoned judgment that explains their decision.[76]

The House of Lords suggested amendments to the bill that would allow for judicial discretion in deciding whether to use a CMP, rather than mandating closed procedures.[77] This allows the judge to balance the competing interests of national security and open justice in the particular circumstances of the case. The government accepted this change, and s. 6(5) of the *Act* provides that the court may allow a closed material application in cases involving sensitive information if "it is in the interests of the fair and effective administration of justice".

The increased use of CMP's and the *Justice and Security Act* are just two more examples of how modern national security concerns test the open court principle. In a time where secrecy is seen as an essential component of national security, is the open court principle sustainable? How can governments and courts reconcile these two competing principles?

III. IS THE OPEN COURTS PRINCIPLE SUSTAINABLE?

Lord Bingham was right to state that the open court principle lies at the heart of the rule of law. As such, we must ensure that our courts conduct their business and render their judgments in public. We do not have to reach back far into history to understand the evil of secret trials and Kafkaesque decrees.

At the same time, we would be foolish not to recognize the pressures that modern society and the communications revolution has placed on the open court principle. We cannot be blind to claims for privacy in the face of ever-more invasive publication practices. Nor can we, since 9/11, ignore the reality that some information must be kept secret for the security of everyone.

[76] Hansard, Report of the 2nd sitting of the House of Lords, November 21, 2012.

[77] *Ibid.*

We must recognize that the open court principle may conflict with other important values, such as privacy or national security. These interests are important to the administration of justice, and only the rash would say that such interests must always yield to the fundamental principle of openness.

The result, as I suggested at the outset, is that as a society – and as a profession – we find ourselves engaged in a new and complicated exercise of line-drawing. No longer can we say that the open court principle prevails, unless the case falls within a handful of circumscribed exceptions. Instead, we must weigh and evaluate the competing interests in context, with the goal of finding a solution that offers adequate protection to privacy and national security, while preserving open justice and the rule of law. Without denying the importance of protecting privacy and security, we must preserve the essential core of the open court principle, and the broader principle of freedom of expression.

How do we do this? In Canada, we have established a common law test for balancing the open court principle against other interests. Judges may limit the open court principle if: 1) such an order is necessary to prevent a serious risk to the proper administration of justice because other reasonably alternative measures will not prevent the risk; and 2) the salutary effects of the limit on openness outweigh the deleterious effects on the rights and interests of the parties and the public.[78]

Drawing the line between conflicting values in the right place is neither an obvious nor easy task. The recent revelations emerging from the Snowden affair have led some to suggest that governments have not always drawn the line between security and privacy in the right place.[79] It is our job as lawyers and judges to ensure that when we are confronted with the task of drawing such lines, we carefully weigh the conflicting concerns in the context at hand. If we do this, I am confident that the open court principle that has sustained the rule of law for the past five hundred years will survive.

[78] *Dagenais v. Canadian Broadcasting Corp*, [1994] 3 S.C.R. 835; *R. v. Mentuck*, 2001 SCC 76, [2001] 3 S.C.R. 442; *Sierra Club of Canada v. Canada (Minister of Finance)*, 2002 SCC 41, [2002] 2 S.C.R. 522; *Toronto Star Newspapers Ltd. v. Ontario*, 2005 SCC 41, [2005] 2 S.C.R. 188.
[79] Ash, *supra*.

The Rule of Law in Times of Turbulence – A Middle Eastern Perspective

HIS EXCELLENCY AWN AL-KHASAWNEH*

Former Vice President of the International Court of Justice
and Prime Minister of Jordan

2 December 2014

At the outset, may I say how delighted I am to be here – in these beautiful and inspiring surroundings – and how honoured to have been invited to address this distinguished and learned audience. My first duty therefore – and it is a pleasant one – is to thank Chantal-Aimée Doerries Q.C., Natalie Darby, Sarah Richardson, Christian Wisskirchen and Jessica Crofts- Lawrence for the kind invitation extended to me and for their hospitality and kind help.

* * *

At the beginning of this year, I started to get "gentle reminders" from the organisers asking me to choose a title for this lecture, but all I could think of was a discouraging sentence in the preface to Lord Bingham's famous book "The Rule of Law", which I had read a few months earlier and which accurately depicted my state of mind at the time; he wrote:

> "The organisers generously offered me a free choice of subject. Such an offer always poses a problem to unimaginative people like myself. We become accustomed at school and university to being given a subject title for our weekly essay, and it was rather the same in legal practice: clients came with specific problems which they wanted answered or appeared before the judge with a specific issue which they wanted (or in some cases did not want) resolved. There was never a free choice of subject-matter."[1]

[1] Tom Bingham, "The Rule of Law", Penguin Books, 2011, p.vii

My life experiences – at least those in the confines of the law- and the habits of mind that such experiences generate (or at least encourage and foster) are only slightly different from those of the late and lamented noble Lord – and hence my similar predicament.

Additionally, when one is addressing such a wise and worldly audience where every single person can, I am sure, sing happily with Ulysses:

> "Much have I seen and known; cities of men And manners, climates, councils, governments, Myself not least…",[2]

the need to say something interesting assumes a certain urgency especially when one is the eighth speaker. Being the eighth speaker is always a problem. It brings to mind the words uttered by Elizabeth Taylor's eighth husband on his wedding night:

> "I know what I am supposed to do tonight but I don't know how to make it more interesting"

Two years ago, Mark Mulholland Q.C. while, speaking in this very hall on the rule of law and global terrorism, made a helpful suggestion as to what the title of the next lecture should be. He said:

> "Joseph Raz in "The Rule of Law and its Virtue" talks of the "promiscuous use" made in recent years of the expression "the rule of law". This concept of promiscuity I must confess intrigues me"[3]

This is Mulholland still speaking. He then went on to say:

> "Berlusconi Bunga Bunga, and the Rule of Law – that is the seventh annual lecture taken care of…" [4]

For my part I confess that no topic can possibly beat that topic for interest- generating, and I hope a future speaker, preferably with first-hand experience, would rise to the challenge. Alas, and I say this with a wistful heart, the life of a Jordanian Prime Minister in office while the phenomenon euphemistically referred to as the Arab Spring, was in full swing, left no time for Bunga Bunga and other joyous frivolities of latter day Romans and their – now deceased – North African Friends.

[2] Alfred lord Tennyson.

[3] Mark Mulholland Q.C., "The Rule of Law & Global Terrorism – an international problem from a Northern Irish perspective", The Bar Council of England& Wales sixth annual International Rule of Law lecture – Inner Temple 18th December 2012, p.4.

[4] Ibid.

Instead I settled on the more demure title of the Rule of Law in Turbulent Times – a Middle Eastern Perspective. In defence of this title, I can confidently assert that it is jammed with action – with a mélange of actors ranging from old oriental potentates, to modern, oriental impotantates – in more senses than one – to single-minded sub-state actors, and I don't speak of charitable organizations or environmentalists, but of groups that aim to restore the *Khilaphate* or to rebuild the Second Temple, or to bring about the end of the world – which is not likely to be a pretty sight. In other words, of fanatics who genuinely want to establish the Rule of Law not in the way Dicey conceived of the concept and Bingham sought to give it content by tying it to recognisable protected interests, but rather in the more literal and dogmatic sense of establishing the rule of *their* law or rather their monolithic interpretation of it. To those groups this is the <u>only</u> meaning of the expression "the Rule of Law"; all else is promiscuous use of language, to borrow again Joseph Raz's sentence.

* * *

Having explained the history of the title, let me now turn to the title itself. Some explanatory words are warranted:

First, I spoke, on purpose, of a Middle Eastern perspective rather than an Arab or a Jordanian perspective because I believe in the essential cultural unity of the region which is not confined to the Arabic-speaking lands but also encompasses countries like Turkey and Iran as well as Pakistan and Afghanistan. The common history, the challenge of the West, the ambivalent national and sub-national identities and the subsequent and closely-related religious revival all attest to a broad cultural homogeneity notwithstanding a mosaic-like diversity.

*

Secondly, I do not propose to detain you too long on futile attempts at finding a waterproof definition of the concept of the rule of law. We have already seen what, in a more pristine sense, the expression means to some groups that believe a society's raison d'être is to live by Islamic law or for that matter, Talmudic law – and I am sure that some fundamentalist Christians espouse identical concepts. To all those groups the rule of law is a simple straight-forward proposition.

Additionally we should not forget that Dicey did not think of the rule of law as a universal principle. He attributed it to specific English institutions and to the role of Judges as opposed to legislative general principles of the constitution. Thus, in a celebrated passage, which I partly quote, he wrote:

"We may say that the constitution [that is the unwritten British constitution] is pervaded by the rule of law on the ground that general principles of the constitution (as for example the right to personal liberty, or the right of public meeting) are with us as a result of judicial decisions determining the rights of private persons in particular cases brought before the courts; whereas under many foreign constitutions the security (such as it is) given to the rights of individuals results, or appears to result, from the general principles of the constitution."[5]

This is a statement with which I am in substantive agreement both with regard to the fact that the concept of the rule of law has a specific and verifiable meaning in the particular historical context of the development of English institutions of which Dicey was rightly proud, and also in regard to the fact that guarantees emphatically made in the constitutions are usually of little value in the absence of long and well-established traditions and a vigilant and courageous judiciary. The perfectly worded constitutions of the now defunct republics of Eastern Europe would attest to this, so would the constitutions of most Arab countries.

The last point I would like to make on the definition of the rule of law, before moving on, is that it defies definition. I do not think Dicey himself expected it to be definable, for he wrote:

"A third and a different sense in which "the rule of law" or the predominance of the legal spirit."

If the rule of law is the equivalent of the predominance of the legal spirit, then it would be well nigh impossible to define: Spirits are notoriously illusive. If forced to define it, I would venture the following eclectic definition:

"The rule of law is the fashionable modern secular response to the concept of justice, especially suited to legal positivism; purged of the intimations of natural law and denuded of overtly moral or theological overtones."

*

The third element in the title, the temporal one, so to speak, is the reference to turbulent times. And this merits some explanation:

[5] Bingham, "The Rule of Law" Penguin Books 2001, p 4.

In point of time, the Middle East is now passing through a tumultuous period, but I cannot think of a time when that region, the cradle of civilization – and this is not a compliment given what modern civilization has been capable of doing – was not passing through tumult and mayhem often resulting in the wholesale annihilation of communities and nations.

The Middle East is littered with archaeological finds chiselling in stone the mighty deeds of bygone despots. Consider please, dear and distinguished audience, the following sample executed at the orders of the Babylonian king Nebuchadnezzar:

> "I have left all of Phoenicia in flames, there is much wailing in Aaram, and in Judea there is lamentation. Damascus has no soul left …etc etc.."

At first glance, no sane person would view those reprehensible acts – seen as mighty deeds by their perpetrators – as contributing to the establishment or the enhancement of the Rule of Law. But in fairness, it must be said that from the point of view of strict legal positivism, Nebuchadnezzar was not breaking any extant law if we take too seriously the maxim *nullum crimen nulla poena sine lege* and certainly not if the word *lex* in the maxim is confined to written law.

This example typifies the predicament of the Middle East and perhaps of the whole world since ancient times: Codes of law, *Hammurabis* being the most famous, coexisting with unspeakable acts of violence and destruction. The Assyrians and Babylonians felt no guilt about killing and there was no need therefore to justify it. This does not mean that they did not have their own concepts of justice and law in domestic matters, for we know that since Akkadian times the notion that the king should obey the law was prevalent in Mesopotamia. According to the Akkadian Omen Series:

> "If a king respects the law, that reign will be long. He will proceed happily."[6]

Other peoples felt the need for justification through divine commandments, a prime example being the destruction of the Midianites by their next of kin the ancient Israelites on direct command from God – twice repeated to Moses for the sake of completeness over a question of worship. One sees in these examples and others a pattern relevant and

[6] From the omen series *Summa Alu*, Zeinab Bahrani, "Rituals of War – The Body and Violence in Mesopotamia", Zone Books 2008, p.101.

ominous for our times. ISIS (so called Islamic state of Iraq and Syria, which has been described as being as Islamic as the Ku Klux Klan is Christian)[7] is basically doing the same to fellow Muslims or Muslims of a different sect and non-Muslims alike before a shocked international public opinion.

Their obsession with destroying ancient monuments is also reminiscent of old obsessions with "graven images" or the "iconoclasm" of medieval Byzantium or the "Wahhabism" of 18th century Arabia.

But the justification may not always be concocted in religious terms, and although I digress a little, I wish to mention briefly the words of Tacitus, the second century Roman historian:

> "They plunder, they slaughter, and they steal: this they falsely name Empire, and where they make a wasteland, they call it peace."[8]

These words always come to mind when I hear talk of the "responsibility to protect", lately fashionable in UN circles or "humanitarian intervention" or worse still, the "establishment of democracy" as justification for intervention in the Middle East.

* * *

I have mentioned all these examples which seem at first glance to have only the remotest connection to the present situation in the Middle East because I can discern patterns whether with regard to the concurrence of the development of legal codes with outbursts of violence or with regard to the justification of war with divine or secular sanction. Be all of these questions as they may, I should restrict myself, given the time limitations, to more recent times and I would propose four periods as important milestones:

1. The *first* is the period of legislative reforms in the Ottoman Empire (the *Tanzimat*) when old concepts of law based on the Shari'a and on ancient traditions were gradually replaced by Western notions of government. Particularly noteworthy is the abandonment of the incremental development of the Shari'a on a judge-by-judge case-by-case basis, along lines similar to the historical development of the common law.

[7] Ambassador Chas W. Freeman, Jr. 23rd "The Collapse of Order in the Middle East Remarks to the 23rd Annual Arab-U.S. Policymakers Conference ", available from http://chasfreeman.net/the-collapse-of-order-in-the-middle-east/ [accessed 7 Dec 2014}

[8] *De vita et moribus Iulii Agricolae,* translation: Loeb Classical Library edition.

Instead that slow and subtle process was replaced by what Lord Bingham referred to as "grand declarations of principle" on the civil law model.[9]

2. The second development was the division of the post-Ottoman Middle East into small and weak sovereignties obsessed with the preservation of existing regimes and hence all sharing similar over-developed security apparatus.

Initially the core of the Middle East – the Fertile Crescent – was placed under class A Mandates by the League of Nations. This was done in implementation of the Wilsonian notion of self-determination which nevertheless applied only to some of the former populations of the defeated Empires, while the infliction of self-determination on the British and French Empires (the so-called process of decolonisation) had to await the outcome of another World War. Ironically, in this surrealistic application of self-determination after World War I, a people who had never been colonised before were to be put under a form of tutelage.

Moreover, in carrying out their duties as mandatory powers, both the British and French governments were not always or often motivated by the declared aim of preserving the interests of the local inhabitants and preparing them for independence (a disguised form of *mission civilitrice*) for which the indigenous populations were less grateful than they were expected to be, as can be gleaned from the numerous revolts which were harshly suppressed and occasioned the first incidence of the use of poison gas.

Additionally, the two Powers were working assiduously from the early 1920s to create favourable conditions for the eventual establishment of the State of Israel in Palestine. This can be discerned for example from the 1923 Paulet-Newcombe agreement on the delimitation of Palestine and Syria, in which it was agreed that the Syrian border would stop 10 meters short of Lake Tiberias. This is like delimiting the boundary of the U.K. to stop a few meters before the sea. The only explanation for this exotic, and as far as I can ascertain, unique, delimitation method is that Lake Tiberias is the sole sweet water reservoir and had to be wholly situated within the Palestinian mandated territory.

However, when one puts aside questions of over-arching imperial policy and the aim of creating favourable conditions for the creation of Israel, the policy of the British Mandate with regard to questions relating to the rule of law at the domestic level was exemplary.

[9] Bingham, "The Rule of Law, p.5.

There was respect for the independence of the judiciary and in Jordan (Trans-Jordan as it was then called) the British administration was notable for being totally free of corruption, efficient, relatively nonintrusive and well tuned to local conditions.

But the old world was shattered – in previous centuries, most of the laws that were applied were not state-made or state-enacted.[10] Rather, they were developed through the jurisprudence of judges and jurists and juris- counsels.

Respected and acknowledged jurists would give opinions following earlier precedents and would distinguish them under certain conditions. Those *fatwas* were collected in compendia and judges drew on them when deciding a case. This process was repeated in every generation and resulted in a *continuous* and *subtle* reinterpretation of the *Shari'a*. By contrast, the legal role of the Caliph or the Sultan was one of occasional legislative intervention coming into play only when called for or when special needs arose.[11] Before going further, let me say that the word *fatwa* nowadays conjures up images of wild-eyed fanatics issuing statements that invariably have something to do with blood-shedding. But many *classical fatwas* were masterpieces of legal reasoning and were noted for humanity and social justice. The jurists and judges in effect became the locus of legitimacy and were often called upon to express the will and aspirations of those belonging to the non-elite classes. In such a milieu, the rule of law assumed a different meaning from those already referred to, and also from the modern liberal democratic meaning of the expression. It meant that the state saw itself as a state *under* the law.

Already in the 19th century, European concepts of government – particularly of the relation of state and law – were permeating the Ottoman Empire and the idea of codification – fashionable in continental Europe – coupled with notions of legal positivism – were prevalent. So a constitution was adopted in 1876 and the tenants of Islamic law were codified in the *Mecelle* between 1869 to 1876, entering into force in 1877.[12]

By the time the Mandates were established this trend had become the norm. The legitimacy of the law was now being sought in the enactments

[10] Occasional legislative action took place in the form of Sultanic orders and Kanons. See in general, Wael Hallaq "An Introduction to Islamic Law".

[11] Wael Hallaq, "An Introduction to Islamic Law", p.40.

[12] The Constitution was influenced by the Belgian Constitution of 1831 and the Prussian Constitution of 1850, see Gabor Agoston and Bruce Masters and , Encyclopedia of the Ottoman Empire, New York 2009.

of the state that passed through a certain legislative process. The impact that this had on the status and quality of judges was enormous. They were reduced to interpreters of the will of the state.

Few people could capture those momentous changes better than Arnold Toynbee. In his seminal "Study of History" he writes:

> "It is a rule and this rule is inherent in the very nature of the declines and falls of civilizations – the demand for codification reaches its climax in the penultimate age before social catastrophe, long after the peak of achievement in jurisprudence has passed, and when the legislators of the day are irretrievably on the run in a losing battle with the ungovernable forces of destruction."[13]

3. I turn now to the <u>third</u> period that is the period of national independence – when the status of judges was dealt a further blow shortly after the end of the Mandate period.

For a short time, the emergence of a sustainable liberal democracy was a possibility in a country like Syria for example, but soon a series of *coups d'état* brought army officers to power, while in Egypt Nasser came to power through a *coup d'état* (in Egypt there is a bad habit of calling every army coup a revolution). There and elsewhere in the Arab world it did not take long before the army officers decided to purge the judiciary; to introduce revolutionary justice; to purport to speak on behalf of the proletariat and the peasants. All power was to be concentrated in the state and the law was now blatantly no more than an instrument of the state – more accurately for those at the helm of the state. Legitimacy was now sought in a tutti-frutti of slogans ranging from liberating Palestine to ideas borrowed from National Socialism, Stalinism, Nationalism and Secularism: concepts that do not sit together well.

The decline in status and relevance of the judiciary was nothing short of disastrous for the rule of law, for I agree with Mark Mulholland Q.C. – earlier quoted on Bunga Bunga – when he says:

> "As once observed by Lord Judge, it is the judges who are the guardians of the rule of law. That is their prime responsibility and in real terms, external vigilance by the judiciary means that they are steadfastly alert for the first incursion by the executive into propriety."

13 Toynbee, "A Study of History", Universal Churches, Vol. 7, London 1954, p.279.

The problem is not specific to the Middle East. Even in a democratic society with established traditions, a government that commands a majority will be tempted to encroach on fundamental liberties and consequently the mettle of which judges are made is put to the test. A telling example was when the late Prime Minister Indira Gandhi introduced restrictive laws especially in the area of preventive detention. In a celebrated case popularly known as the *habeas corpus* case, the more senior judges of the Supreme Court of India ruled in favour of the State's right for unrestricted powers of detention during emergency. The only dissent came from Justice HR Khanna, who stated:

> "Detention without trial is an anathema to all those who love personal liberty…a dissent is an appeal to the brooding spirit of the law, to the intelligence of a future day, when a lack of decision may possibly correct the error into which the dissenting judge believes the Court to have been betrayed."

That dissent cost Justice Khanna the chief justiceship to which he was entitled by convention. But he became a legendary figure among the legal fraternity in India.

The *New York Times* wrote of his opinion:

> "Submission of an independent judiciary to absolute government is virtually the last step in the destruction of a democratic society."

Happily, the Indian Supreme Court has since contributed much in upholding, indeed expanding the basic rights of Indian citizens. How I wish there were more justices like Judge Khanna in the Middle East. My sense of sadness is all the more acutely felt because the history of this region is replete with anecdotes about judges and jurists who didn't hesitate even at great peril to themselves to stand up to sword-yielding despots.

I shall mention only one episode before moving on to our present times, for this episode seems unique in showing the courage and at the same time the immense prestige that judges and jurists enjoyed.

In 1258 Hulagu, Genghis Khan's grandson, captured Baghdad and brought the Abbasid Caliphate, which was a universal state, to an end. The Mongols then ravaged Syria and sent a letter to the Mamluks of Egypt threatening the same consequences as they had visited on numerous cities and lands if they did not surrender,

The Mamluks, who were Central Asian Turkish slaves and had become the masters of Egypt, were acutely short of money to raise an army to meet the Mongols; they turned to the preeminent jurist of his time, Ibn Abdulsalam, for a legal opinion, a *fatwa,* permitting them to impose new taxes. (Islamic law does not permit the imposition of any new taxation unless there is no other way – President Reagan would have been very happy had he lived in those times, except of course for the looming Mongol threat). The old jurist, Ibn Abdulsalam, would not give an opinion unless the leading Mamluk princes sold all the gold and silver they had accumulated and unless those of them who were nominally slaves of the public treasury were manumitted in a public auction that actually took place over their protests.

Only then did he issue that opinion to raise new taxes. In the same year, the Mamluks defeated the Mongols at Ain Jalut (Goliath's Spring) in a victory that changed world history.

There are many lessons for our times from that episode; especially when we consider how the claims of external threats and national emergencies flow too easily from the official mouth.[14]

Three years ago, when President Mursi of Egypt, rather ineptly and unwisely, granted himself sweeping powers in the interim period until a new constitution was in place, the top judges of Egypt condemned this move as an attack on the independence of the judiciary. I thought at the time that the old fire that Ibn Abdelsalam had lit almost seven hundred years ago had not been totally extinguished; or that those judges were perchance inspired by Judge Khanna or by the jurisprudence of British courts – decisions like the *Belmarsh* case are widely consulted and admired. My happiness, however, was short-lived; for later when a *coup d'état* brought the army back to power the very same judges with notable and rare exceptions became the epitome of compliance and subservience when draconian powers were taken by the military in comparison to which Morsi's ill-advised decree pales. Today the judiciary of Egypt is sadly an instrument of a state not known for its subtlety: condemning youths to long prison sentences for peaceful demonstration and, earlier this year, sentencing in a summary trial 528 persons to death.[15]

We are all agreed that the independence of the judiciary is a *conditio sine qua non* for the efficacy of the rule of law. But what if the judges have

[14] A variation on the famous line by Hafiz of Shiraz: "they flow too easily from the mouth, the words of love." Arberry, "Fifty Poems of Hafiz" Cambridge University Press, 1974.

[15] The UN has described this rise in conviction as "unprecedented".

been appointed by a police state or a corrupt regime? What if they are part of what is commonly known as the "deep state"?

Sir Sydney Kentridge Q.C. wrote:

> "It [the independence of the judiciary] is secured in part by laws which give judges security of tenure, and in part by insuring as far as possible that they are persons of integrity, appointed on merit rather than by reason of political connection."

There is a dilemma here and ultimately no matter how much we praise the courage of individual judges, the rule of law depends also on the concurrent commitment of the government; on the awareness of the populous – when the Mamluks of Egypt initially – and understandably – refused to be publicly auctioned – Ibn Abdulsalam left Cairo and most of the population followed him until the ruling class relented.

The rule of law also depends on the existence of a robust Bar. I was gratified, as a matter of professional commitment, to read about the action (*action directe*) that the Bar Council, the Law Society, and the Chartered Institute of Legal Executives took, six days ago by writing to MPs urging them to protect judicial review.

The rule of law can also be severely curtailed, indeed undermined, by legislation. Consider for example a constitutional article stipulating that the right of peaceful assembly is guaranteed in accordance with the law when no law exists at the time or when the law in question is vague. Such texts exist in most Arab constitutions including the Jordanian constitution. Or consider general statements cast as constitutional provisions like: torture is prohibited, and evidence obtained through torture is inadmissible in a court of law. The value of such a provision would only be real if the law were to shift the *onus probandi* to the state to prove that there was no torture; if the law were to provide for investigations into allegations of torture and compensation for victims of torture. A very dangerous practice also is the drafting of criminal law texts in general and elastic formulae that defy objective verification. A comic/tragic example is article 118/2 of the Jordanian Penal Code that criminalises an action "that disturbs relations with a foreign state".

In many cases in the Middle East such texts are drafted by the security services and sent to rubber stamp parliaments. When the state thinks of legal reform as no more than a *vitrine* to impress the outside world this means that it has abdicated its responsibility to uphold justice. And there is little that the judges can do to ameliorate the situation.

The contrary is true, the Human Rights Act of 1998 is thought by many commentators to have been responsible for the fact that the House of Lords adopted a different approach in the Belmarsh case from the traditional one where courts had been generally unwilling to second-guess the government, when it asserted that some step or another had to be taken to uphold national security.

* * *

4. Let me now turn to the present period, the fourth milestone as I had termed it in an attempt to give some temporal structure to this lecture, and which I fear may have become lost to wayfarers due to my many digressions. Under this heading, I shall deal with the impact of terrorism, the so-called War on Terrorism, also dubbed the war to establish democracy in the Middle East, which reminds me of what the Duke of Wellington famously said:

"If you believe that, you'll believe anything."

This war has been going on at least since the Soviet invasion of Afghanistan, and consisted mostly of covert (and sometimes not so covert) action by Cold War warriors intent on seizing a golden chance to hasten the collapse of a Soviet Union already perceived by incisive observers as *l'empire eclatée*.[16] The first mujahideen were mostly romantics like those who travelled to fight in the Spanish Civil War. President Reagan was generous with his praise, even comparing them with the founding fathers of the United States.[17] "What went wrong?", to use the words of Bernard Lewis. First, they splintered into sectarian groups after the defeat of the Soviets, intent on killing fellow Muslims of a different sect. This deviation owed its reasons to regional rivalries and to indoctrination. Secondly, the reality and horror of war transforms people, as you have learned in this country and in the United States from the experience of returning soldiers. Any sane and humane society seeks to rehabilitate its errant sons. But the abandonment of Afghanistan and its people was matched only by the abandonment of those persons by their own countries. And they became the object of suspicion and ill-treatment by regimes that thought they could do business as before without taking notice of the fundamental changes that have taken place in the world and in their societies. Herein lies, I think, a partial explanation for subsequent and horrendous events.

16 Hélène Carrère d`Encausse, "L'empire Eclatée", Flammarion, 1978.

17 Remarks at the Annual Dinner of the Conservative Political Action Conference March 1, 1985.

With the coming of the neo-conservatives to power in the United States, espousing a grand project to turn the existing informal American empire of the world into a formal one, which to them had become "*do-able*", the so-called War on Terror became an inevitability.[18] The atrocity committed on 11 September 2001 turned this war into a open and full-fledged one.

In this war, a new jargon was developed, and to a lawyer it was not a pleasant sounding one. The very titles betrayed malice aforethought to the rule of law: regime change, secret prisons, collateral damage, not going down the UN path, creative chaos, reliable intelligence, extraordinary rendition, enhanced interrogation techniques. Few would also doubt that the neo-conservatives held the rule of law in contempt, at the international level for sure, but also their own law seen by them as no more than an obstacle to be circumvented by clever lawyers, the extra-territoriality of Guantanamo being a prime example.

When the law did not permit them to carry out particularly egregious acts – for we should not forget that the United States has a long tradition of espousing the rule of law – they turned to their friends and allies to do the dirtier work for them. Unfortunately, there were too many who were too eager to oblige.

To the intelligence community in the Middle East and elsewhere, the war on terror proved a bonanza. In his book "Plan of Attack",[19] Bob Woodward explains how money flowed to regional Middle Eastern intelligence services. Equally ominously, this war was a chance for this fraternity to permeate all aspects of life, in effect to become the masters of the state and not the servants of the state., By contrast, the War on Terror, exposed the local population to unspeakable horrors, particularly in Afghanistan and Iraq and now Syria. In Iraq alone it is estimated that there are five million orphans, "collateral damage" in the parlance of imperial hubris. Very few of the damaged have been able to obtain redress, except in a few notable and laudable cases before British – and Canadian – courts. But how many people have access to such courts? In the Middle East itself, restrictive laws, jurisdictional obstacles, the absence of compensatory provisions in existing laws and the simple poverty of the people have effectively insured impunity to servicemen and, worse still, to mercenaries, also called, in the new Orwellian language, subcontractors.

[18] James P. Pfiffner, Mark Phythian, "Intelligence and National Security Policymaking on Iraq: British and American Perspectives", Texas, 2008 p.32 {emphasis added]

[19] Woodward, "Plan of Attack", Simon & Schuster 2004.

In the meanwhile, the terrorists have metamorphosed from fighters against the "Evil Empire" into nihilists fighting against themselves, and against religious minorities that have lived peacefully under the protection of Islam for over fourteen centuries. Their interpretation of Islam makes the blood curdle, for they have reduced a great civilisation to an obsession with bloodshed and cruel punishments. Almost every week a woman or a man is stoned for adultery. Ibn Al Atheer, the great Medieval Arab historian, wrote a history of Baghdad after its fall to the Moguls. The following sentence is taken from his famous history:

> "In that year a woman was stoned in Baghdad for adultery, thus bringing to three the number of women thus stoned since the foundation of Baghdad." – in other words, in 500 years.

The choices facing ordinary people in the Middle East are very difficult. I am always reminded of the imperishable words of Yeats in his great poem "The Second Coming":

> "The best lack all conviction, while the worst are full of passionate intensity."

To complete this picture let me remind you that there are people, Jews and gentiles alike, who are currently searching for a calf with some unique bodily characteristics as a sign to rebuild the Second Temple in Jerusalem – obviously we have no monopoly on fanatics. While with similar passionate intensity the building of illegal settlements and the adoption of increasingly racist laws and measures continues, the chances of a dignified peace in the Holy Land have all but evaporated.

* * *

We may conclude from this dim picture that the rule of law is not in the best of health in the Middle East, nor that it is the uppermost consideration on the minds of ordinary citizens. I doubt whether it ever was on the minds of those at the helm of power. Instead, what seems to be on the minds of everyone are eschatological expectations and millenialistic concepts ominously shared – though in slightly different versions – by the three monotheistic religions.

As I contemplate the present untenable situation in the Middle East, I feel we are watching a replay of the "Eastern Question" – that period in the second half of the 19th century when threats and diplomacy characterised European Powers' dealings with the Ottoman Empire and their increasing intervention into its internal affairs – with the important difference that the over-arching empire has been replaced by weak sovereignties obsessed with security.

* * *

What we see now in the Middle East is not only the result of recent events. It has its roots in classical and Biblical history and more recently in the replacement of an old tradition of government and law by an imported and alien one. The net result of this has been the reduction of the judiciary, who had been the cornerstone in upholding the respect for the rule of law, into state functionaries (*petits fonctionnaires*), notwithstanding the grand declarations in various constitutions about the independence of the judiciary. In the past few decades, the War on Terror and the concurrent decline in efficacy of small and weak states and the constant interference from outside, have brought the rule of law to new depths.

But this, I feel, is an aberration. If we are shackled, we are shackled not by the past but by the present. I have devoted a considerable part of this lecture to the history of the area as a *correctif* to the commonly-held but mistaken idea that what we see today is a reflection of our tradition and history.

At first glance, it may seem, especially as we contemplate the fate that has befallen the Arab Spring, that we are in that state best described by Matthew Arnold in his great poem, "Stanzas from the Grande Chartreuse" as

> "wandering between two worlds, one dead, the other powerless to be born".

I can only hope that in its long history; in its past cosmopolitanism; in its ability to rise again – phoenix-like – after disasters, that the Middle East region will find an inspiration to walk back from the abyss. For all the complexity of the problems, the profundity of the challenges and the malaise that permeates the region, I still find solace and hope in the poetry of Hafiz of Shiraz:

> "Joseph is back in the land of Canaan
> A little changed by the passage of time
> But he is back so have no fear
> And in this house of sadness there is a rock on which a rose will bloom
> So have no fear."

On this happier note, I wish to thank you all for your patience.

Strength and Fragility in Tandem: The Rule of Law in Hong Kong

HON CHIEF JUSTICE GEOFFREY MA

Chief Justice of Hong Kong

11 May 2015

It is 40 years almost to the day since I last spoke in this Hall. It was then a mooting competition between universities. I remember talking about exemption clauses, *Suisse Atlantique*[1] and *Lep Air Services*.[2] That evening, I spoke in front of nine Benchers including Lord Cross of Chelsea, Lord Edmund Davies, Mr Michael Mustill QC[3] and others. This evening the task is a challenging one because the topic is one that is critical in Hong Kong, has been for a number of years (indeed ever since 1 July 1997) and will continue to be so. The rule of law is seen by many as being Hong Kong's strength and regarded by some as an economic advantage enjoyed over the rest of China, indeed the whole of the South East Asia region. And yet, seemingly increasingly so in the light of recent events, it has been called into question. One asks rhetorically: is the rule of law in Hong Kong really so fragile that it starts to totter in the wake of certain events? Or is it in reality a strong institution, one of the cornerstones of Hong Kong's success?

Much of course depends on what those events are and recent events over the past year in Hong Kong provide useful case studies in order to illustrate broader considerations:-

(1) The Occupy protests in Hong Kong which lasted 79 days last year from September to December.[4] The protests effectively

[1] *Suisse Atlantique Societe d'Armement SA v NV Rotterdamsche Kolen Centrale* [1967] 1 AC 361

[2] *Lep Air Services Ltd v Rolloswin Investments Ltd* [1973] AC 331.

[3] The late Lord Mustill.

[4] The flyer to this evening incorporates a photograph of the protesters occupying main roads in the centre of Hong Kong. The equivalent in London would be the occupation of

ended when injunctions were ordered by the court arising out of private law suits based on public nuisance initiated by nearby building owners, and bus and taxi operators. The concerns expressed regarding the rule of law were that the protestors, although they were legally represented in the court proceedings, did not comply with the injunctions ordered by the court, waiting instead until the bailiffs enforced the court orders before vacating the streets.

(2) The White Paper published in June 2014 stated the views of the State Council of the PRC[5] regarding the constitutional model for Hong Kong of "one country two systems". Of particular note were the references to judges being "administrators" and having to be "patriotic". This was viewed as affecting the rule of law in that it indicated an attempt to undermine the independence of the Judiciary.

(3) Pressure groups and others including legislators have continually been complaining publicly about the acquittal of persons prosecuted in the Occupy protests. The concerns over the rule of law are that the courts, by acquitting the persons charged, have been acting inconsistently with public opinion and against the public interest.

These incidents have called into question the existence of the rule of law in Hong Kong, as to whether it really exists, at least whether it has been undermined. And what of the future: even if the rule of law now prevails in Hong Kong, is there a risk that it will only become increasingly eroded? These are relevant questions, justified and relevant not least because they are of genuine concern to Hong Kong people. If the Hong Kong community regards the rule of law as a fragile institution, this is obviously of some concern because the existence of the rule of law and its legitimacy in any community is entirely dependent on the respect in that community for the concept as a core value of society.

Before addressing these points in the context of the events earlier mentioned, we must first agree on just what the concept of the rule of law means. The lectures previously delivered by those illustrious jurists in the Bar's Annual International Rule of Law Lectures have referred to "The

Piccadilly in the West End or Bishopsgate and Cannon Street in the City.

[5] Under Article 85 of the Constitution of the People's Republic of China, the State Council is the executive body of the highest organ of state power and is the highest organ of state administration.

Rule of Law" by Lord Bingham of Cornhill[6] and I will do likewise. I always consult two books first whenever I am asked to speak about the rule of law: Lord Bingham's book, and the inspirational collection of lectures and talks given by Sir Sydney Kentridge QC contained in "Free Country".[7] In his lecture on the Rule of Law: Ideals and Realities,[8] Sir Sydney pays tribute to Lord Bingham's book, to Lord Bingham himself[9] and says it is the starting point for any discussion on the subject.[10]

In the Rule of Law, after referring to well-known quotations from works of Shakespeare[11] and Dickens[12] basically disparaging lawyers, Lord Bingham had this to say about the rule of law:-

> "But belief in the rule of law does not import unqualified admiration of the law, or the legal profession, or the courts, or the judges. We can hang on to most of our prejudices. It does, however, call on us to accept that we would very much rather live in a country which complies, or at least seeks to comply, with the principle I have stated than in one which does not. The hallmarks of a regime which flouts the rule of law are, alas, all too familiar: the midnight knock on the door, the sudden disappearance, the show trial, the subjection of prisoners to genetic experiment, the confession extracted by torture, the gulag and the concentration camp, the gas chamber, the practice of genocide or ethnic cleansing, the waging of aggressive war. The list is endless. Better to put up with some choleric judges and greedy lawyers."[13]

In his lecture on the Rule of Law to which I have just referred, Sir Sidney Kentridge recounted an incident in post- Apartheid South Africa in 1998.[14] The President of South Africa, Nelson Mandela, had appointed a judicial commission to inquire into allegations that the administration of rugby in the country was corrupt and operated on nepotism. He was sued by the person who was then in charge of the sport.[15] It was alleged

6 Allen Lane, 2010.

7 Hart Publishing, 2012.

8 Delivered at the 17th Commonwealth Law Conference held in February 2011 in Hyderabad. Reproduced in Free Country at page 147-158.

9 A "truly noble and humane judge": Free Country at page 158.

10 Free Country at page 148.

11 Henry VI, Part II spoken by Dick the Butcher: "The first thing we do, let's kill all the lawyers".

12 Oliver Twist said by Mr Bumble: "If the law supposes that … the law is an ass".

13 The Rule of Law at page 9.

14 Free Country at page 150.

15 He was the President of the South African Rugby Football Union.

that the President had failed to consider the matter himself (as required by statute), instead merely rubber-stamping the recommendation made by a minister. President Mandela swore an affidavit in which he stated he had made the decision after full personal consideration of the matter. It was, however, not left there. The judge[16] ordered the President to be cross-examined on his affidavit. This no doubt caused much shock to laymen and lawyers alike. No attempt, however, was made by President Mandela to appeal the judge's order nor did he claim executive privilege. However resentful he was at what appeared to many to be an affront to the Office of the President of South Africa, President Mandela stated that an order of the court had to be obeyed by every person. He therefore took the stand on 19th March 1998 and was, aged 79, cross-examined for five hours during which time he stood in the witness stand declining to sit and answering all questions with dignity and courtesy. As Sir Sydney describes, "This was a leader demonstrating to his country the meaning of the rule of law".

The reason why I have extracted passages from these two books is to lend some backing to what I hope is a simple but accurate definition of the rule of law and it is a definition which I have often used as a foundation of any discussion on this topic. For me, the rule of law encapsulates two important but related concepts:- first, there must exist laws which respect the dignity, rights and liberties of the individual in any society and secondly, there must exist an independent institution which enforces rights, liberties and freedoms both in letter and, more important, in spirit. There is nothing original in this definition which I adopt: the two facets of the rule of law constitute in essence the lasting themes of Magna Carta.[17]

The first facet is a reference to the contents of the law. In the legal system with which most persons in this Hall are familiar and which is the legal system in Hong Kong – the common law system – the laws are contained of course in statutes, in the case of Hong Kong in a constitution (the Basic Law) as well and also in the cases decided by the courts which form the vast body of what are called legal precedents. The importance of case law in the common law system cannot be downplayed. It is case law that reflects the true spirit of the law. The reference to dignity may at first

[16] William de Villiers.

[17] See Lady Justice Arden's essay "Magna Carta and the Judges: Why Magna Carta matters" contained in Magna Carta, Muse and Mentor (Thomson Reuters, Library of Congress, 2014) at page 181-189. As Arden LJ says "Magna Carta is a monumental affirmation of the rule of law".

seem odd given the vagueness of the term. It is, however, a recognized concept in the human rights context. Thus, we see the word "dignity" used in a number of modern constitutions, [18] in the Preamble to the Charter of the United Nations (1945) and the Universal Declaration of Human Rights (1948), in human rights conventions such as the International Covenant on Civil and Political Rights (1966) ("ICCPR"). The nature of dignity as a right, and this reflects the spirit of the law, was articulated by Justice Kate O'Regan of the Constitutional Court of South Africa in *Dawood v Minister of Home Affairs*[19]:-

> "The value of dignity in our Constitutional framework cannot therefore be doubted. The Constitution asserts dignity to contradict our past in which human dignity for black South Africans was routinely and cruelly denied. It asserts it too to inform the future, to invest in our democracy respect for the intrinsic worth of all human beings. Human dignity therefore informs constitutional adjudication and interpretation at a range of levels. It is a value that informs the interpretation of many, possibly all, other rights."

The second part of my definition is a direct reference to an independent judiciary enforcing the law both in letter and in spirit. One may perhaps sometimes take this for granted and it certainly reflects the reality in many places – I certainly believe Hong Kong is such a place – but perceptions are important. A judiciary, even if in reality truly independent but which is not perceived as being independent, loses the confidence of the community and has its work cut out to convince the population that it truly does deliver what is expected of it. It is easy to see why. If the rule of law is a cohesive force which binds a society enabling it to function as such, a lack of respect for it will obviously undermine this essential cohesion.

And so I return to the recent events in Hong Kong earlier outlined. Do they indicate that the rule of law in Hong Kong is at risk? Certainly, the spotlight is on the rule of law but do these incidents demonstrate a fragility in its existence? In order properly to answer these questions, one of course needs to refer back to the definition of the rule of law and asks what I think is the fundamental question to be asked: how does one show objectively and empirically whether or not the

[18] Such as in Germany, Israel, South Africa and Switzerland. Section 10 of the Constitution of South Africa states the constitutional right as follows: "Everyone has inherent dignity and the right to have their dignity respected". The jurisprudence on dignity is advanced and plentiful in Germany and South Africa.

[19] 200 (3) SA 936.

rule of law exists in any place? I will attempt to do so largely by reference to the position in Hong Kong. Only when this fundamental question is satisfactorily answered can a community start to have a respect for the law and the rule of law. So how does one go about proving the existence of the rule of law?

I ought to start by discussing a factor which, in my view, should be irrelevant to answering the fundamental question:- merely looking at the outcome of cases that go before the court.

This is the fallacy that underlies most discussions on the rule of law, as to whether it exists or not. Many people including many lawyers and legal academics, however, regard the result of cases as a reliable barometer. A ready and simple example of this can be found in public law cases: whenever the government loses a case, it is said that the rule of law is alive and well; the opposite when the government wins. In a case decided by the Court of Final Appeal last year[20] in which it was held that persons who were in the position of mandated refugees[21] and the screened-in torture claimants[22] did not have the constitutional right to work whilst in Hong Kong, immediately after the handing down of the judgment of the court, the lawyer for the unsuccessful applicants faced the media and was reported to have said that the judgment was "an embarrassment for the legal system" in Hong Kong. Similar sentiments are expressed by pro-government groups when the result of court cases goes against the government. In a case determined by the Court of Final Appeal in 2013,[23] the court held that the Government had failed to satisfy the proportionality test in its policy to restrict social security assistance to persons who have resided in Hong Kong for a minimum of seven years (in practical terms this policy excluded many new immigrants from the Mainland). This led to groups of Hong Kong residents demonstrating their dissatisfaction in the streets. Assertions that the rule of law had been undermined by the court were made. In the third case study referred to earlier where pressure groups complain about the acquittal of persons involved in the Occupy protests, it is clear that when it is said that the rule of law is undermined, what is really meant is that the outcome of the cases has not been to certain people's liking. And yet, if one is analyzing

20 *GA v Director of Immigration* (2014) 17 HKCFAR 60.

21 Persons who have established their claims as refugees under the 1951 United Nations Convention Relating to the Status of Refugees, together with the 1967 Protocol.

22 Claimants who have established themselves as torture claimants under the Convention Against Torture and Other Cruel, Inhuman or Degrading Treatment or Punishment.

23 *Kong Yunming v Director of Social Welfare* (2013) 16 HKCFAR 950.

cases determined by the courts, the more pertinent question must of course surely be whether the court has applied the law and acted in accordance with law, as opposed to applying extraneous factors (meaning non-legal matters such as political considerations). Put shortly, the existence or non-existence of the rule of law cannot be gauged by the outcome of a case alone. After all, and this is particularly so in public law cases, the individual parties or a portion of the public (even the majority) may wish for a particular result, but whether or not the result is achieved is entirely dependent on the legal merits, and the result alone provides no clue as to whether the court has acted independently or in accordance with its constitutional mandate of applying the law and its spirit, and nothing else. It is perhaps convenient that this point to make reference also to the Judicial Oath in Hong Kong[24] which requires a judge to uphold the law, act in full accordance with the law, and safeguard the law and administer justice without fear or favour, self-interest or deceit.

In looking for objective indications of the existence of the rule of law comprising the two facets earlier identified, one starts with an examination of the legal infrastructure in place; in other words, the position on paper. This requires mainly looking at the protections guaranteed under the relevant constitution (if there is one) and relevant statutes.

In Hong Kong, by no means unique in this regard, we find the following. Reference can conveniently be made to the Basic Law of the Hong Kong Special Administrative Region, which, as I have said earlier, is Hong Kong's own constitution.[25]

The Basic Law contains the following important provisions: -

(1) The independence of the Judiciary is set out in three different provisions: Articles 2, 19 and 85.

(2) Fundamental rights are expressly set out: equality before the law;[26] the right to vote and stand for elections;[27] freedom of speech, of the press and publication, freedom of association, of assembly, of procession and of demonstration, the right and freedom to form and join trade unions and to strike;[28] freedom of conscience;[29]

[24] Similar in wording to all oaths commonly taken by all judges in most jurisdictions.
[25] This year is the 25th anniversary of the promulgation of the Basic Law, although it did not take effect until 1 July 1997.
[26] Article 25.
[27] Article 26.
[28] Article 27.
[29] Article 32.

the right to access to the courts;[30] the right to social welfare;[31] the freedom of marriage.[32]

(3) Article 39 is of immense importance. That article provides that the ICCPR (mentioned earlier)[33] as applied to Hong Kong shall be in force and implemented through the laws in Hong Kong. The ICCPR is implemented in Hong Kong[34] through the Hong Kong Bill of Rights Ordinance,[35] which reproduces almost word for word the provisions of the Convention. Thus, one finds contained in Hong Kong's Bill of Rights, the right to equal treatment (Articles 1 and 22), the right not to be subject to torture or to cruel, inhuman or degrading treatment or punishment (Article 3), the right not to be held in slavery or servitude (Article 4), freedom of thought, conscience and religion (Article 15), the right to hold opinions without interference and the right to freedom of expression (Article 16), the right of peaceful assembly (Article 17), the right to freedom of association (Article 18), and other rights.

(4) Article 8 states that the laws in force in Hong Kong prior to 1 July 1997, that is, "the common law, rules of equity, ordinances, subordinate legislation and customary law" are to be maintained. Article 18 reiterates this. Article 81 states that the judicial system previously practised in Hong Kong shall be maintained. Article 82 provides that the Court of Final Appeal in Hong Kong may as required invite judges from other common law jurisdictions to sit on the Court of Final Appeal.[36] In the adjudication of cases, Hong Kong courts can refer to precedents of other common law jurisdictions (Article 84). Apart from the Chief Justice and the Chief Judge of the High Court, who must be Chinese citizens

30 Article 35.

31 Article 36.

32 Article 37.

33 See para. 8 above.

34 This is necessary to give effect to the Convention under the common law dualist principle (that international treaties are not self-executing unless made part of domestic law by legislation): *Ubamaka v Secretary for Security* (2012) 15 HKCFAR 743, at para. 43.

35 Cap. 383.

36 In every substantive appeal (except one) heard by the Court of Final Appeal since the Court was established on 1 July 1997, the Court has included a judge from another common law jurisdiction. There are at present twelve judges, called Non-Permanent Judges, on the panel of judges from other common law jurisdictions:- Australia: Sir Anthony Mason, Justice Murray Gleeson, Justice James Spigelman, Justice William Gummow; England: Lord Hoffmann, Lord Millett, Lord Neuberger of Abbotsbury, Lord Walker of Gestingthorpe, Lord Collins of Mapesbury, Lord Clarke of Stone-cum-Ebony, Lord Phillips of Worth Matravers; and New Zealand: Sir Thomas Munro Gault.

who are permanent residents of Hong Kong with no right of abode elsewhere, there are no nationality restrictions for any other judge in Hong Kong (Article 90). Judges are to be appointed only on the basis of their judicial and professional qualities and judges may be recruited from other common law jurisdictions (Article 92). I have mentioned these provisions to make one point: that Hong Kong is a common law jurisdiction, together with all the obligations, characteristics and judicial approach that this entails.

(5) Finally, in relation to the Basic Law, I would draw attention to Article 11 which states in part that "no law enacted by the legislature of the Hong Kong Special Administrative Region shall contravene this law". Further, section 6 of the Hong Kong Bill of Rights Ordinance provides that where there is a violation of any of the provisions in the Bill of Rights, a court can grant any relief which it considers appropriate and just. These provisions in the Basic Law and in the Ordinance empower the courts to declare statutes void if held to be unconstitutional. This is not a power that exists in many jurisdictions, the United Kingdom and New Zealand included.

I now deal with the second – and more important – half of the exercise to demonstrate, objectively, that the rule of law exists. Put bluntly, it really amounts to this: even with what I have referred to as a sound legal infrastructure exists, is the position on paper matched by the reality? In other words: do the courts in reality protect fundamental rights and are they truly independent?

After all, we have all had experience of some jurisdictions which, on the surface, have acceptable laws in place but where, sadly, the reality differs, sometimes dramatically.

In my view, there are six factors which are relevant to this exercise.

First, transparency of the legal system. The idea of open justice whereby most court proceedings are open to the public to observe,[37] is an obvious indication of the rule of law. The fact that any member of the public is able to observe court proceedings provides an effective supervision of the whole of the judicial process. Closely connected to this is the ability, save in exceptional and recognized circumstances, of the press to report.

37 Save for the most sensitive cases, such as certain matrimonial proceedings (especially where children are concerned) or Mareva injunctions or Anton Piller orders.

This is embodied in Article 14.1 of the ICCPR (Article 10 of the Hong Kong Bill of Rights)[38] and is a common characteristic of common law jurisdictions.

Secondly and this for me provides a crucial indication of the existence of the rule of law, the reasoned judgments. This is an important characteristic of the common law. Reasoned decisions demonstrate not only to the parties to the particular suit but also to the world at large, the precise thought process of the court in arriving at any decision. It exposes for detailed analysis and scrutiny the reasons for a decision and, where these reasons are not convincing, the judgment will enable the losing party to consider an appeal. In jury trials, there is of course no requirement on a jury to provide reasons but a jury's verdict is always preceded by a detailed summing-up, from which one can often work out the reasons to justify or explain a jury's verdict. A reasoned judgment will demonstrate that a court has discharged its responsibility of determining the outcome of cases strictly according to law, and legal principles, and has acted independently. Put another way, where the decision of a court is not accompanied by any reasons at all or wholly inadequate reasons, this may give rise to speculation as to whether a court has really acted strictly according to the law or whether it has instead taken into account extraneous and illegitimate factors. Of course, it does not follow that where judgments do not contain reasons or have inadequate reasons that the court is not independent but certainly, the existence of the reasoned judgments will go a long way to dispel any such speculation. And if the relevant proceedings are behind closed doors, adverse speculation is even more intense.

Thirdly, connected to the second factor just discussed, a reasoned judgment will indicate clearly the court's approach to the law. In the area of human rights, one can then see the approach of the court as to whether human rights are generously construed and applied, or not. In Hong Kong, numerous cases, some of which have resulted in statutory provisions being declared void for unconstitutionality, have stated and reiterated that in dealing with fundamental rights, they are to be purposively and generously interpreted so as to give persons the full benefit of constitutionally guaranteed fundamental rights and freedoms.[39] Correspondingly, any restrictions on rights should be

38 Public hearings and the requirement that judgments be made public.

39 This point was emphasized early on in the judgments of the Court of Final Appeal. See, for example, *Ng Ka Ling v Director of Immigration* (1999) 2 HKCFAR 4, at 28-29.

narrowly construed. There is nothing surprising or controversial in this approach; it is in line with other common law jurisdictions.

Fourthly, the appointment process of judges is also a relevant consideration in determining the independence of the Judiciary. I have already referred earlier to that provision in the Basic Law which mandates the judges should be appointed on the basis of their judicial and professional qualities. The appointment procedure in Hong Kong is that although the Chief Executive[40] formally appoints judges, he does so on the recommendation of an independent commission comprising judges, members of the legal profession and lay persons.[41] Removal of judges at District Court level and above can only be by reason of inability to discharge his or her duties or misbehaviour, and only on the recommendation of a tribunal appointed by the Chief Justice consisting of no fewer than three judges; in the case of the Chief Justice, a tribunal appointed by the Chief Executive consisting of no fewer than five judges.[42] For judicial officers below the level of the District Court (magistrates), they can be removed only by reason of inability to discharge duties or misbehavior after an investigation by a tribunal comprising two High Court judges and a public officer.[43] Removal is by the Chief Executive on the recommendation of the Judicial Officers Recommendation Commission.

I mentioned as one of the concerns about the rule of law in Hong Kong the White Paper published in June last year.[44] The concerns were over the reference to judges as "administrators" and having to be "patriotic". These remarks were seen to be an interference or undermining of judicial independence. For me, quite simply, whatever was intended, meant or not meant, the constitutional and legal position is as stipulated under the Basic Law in the provisions I have identified. They state and reiterate clearly the independence of the Judiciary in Hong Kong. And the reality matches this. At the end of the day, the meaning of a word can be debated endlessly. As Lord Neuberger of Abbotsbury said in a speech he delivered in Hong Kong[45] when discussing the same issue "Well, like many legal issues, the argument is ultimately about the meaning of a word, and words are slippery things."

[40] The head of the Government in Hong Kong.

[41] Article 88 of the Basic Law. The relevant commission in Hong Kong is the Judicial Officers Recommendation Commission.

[42] Article 89 of the Basic Law.

[43] See the Judicial Officers (Tenure of Office) Ordinance Cap 433.

[44] Para 2 (2) above.

[45] "The Third and Fourth Estates: Judges, Journalists and Open Justice" delivered on 26 August 2014 at the Hong Kong Foreign Correspondents' Club.

What is more important is a recognition of fundamentals. One might say judges administer the law or are patriotic to their jurisdiction, but what this does not mean is that in the discharge of their judicial function, they will be somehow partial or biased towards anyone or anything.

Fifthly, effective access to the courts or justice. The second facet of the rule of law, namely, the existence of an independent institution (the court) to enforce laws, implicitly carries with it the necessity of ensuring effective access to justice. The Occupy movement in Hong Kong effectively ended when the court granted injunctions to remove the protesters from the streets. But the protesters had their day in court and argued their case at length, albeit eventually unsuccessfully. They were all represented by teams of experienced counsel, with a number of leading counsel as well. All except perhaps one or two were on legal aid. This is not the occasion to go into legal aid in detail, whether in Hong Kong or elsewhere. The only point I wish to make is that in Hong Kong, the availability of legal aid is deemed to be an important factor in ensuring access to justice.

Sixthly and lastly, and this is perhaps the most nebulous factor in relation to the determination of the existence of the rule of law, the views of the users of the courts (mainly being perhaps the lawyers) towards the courts and their confidence in the system, provide some indication to support (or, as the case may be, not support) the existence of the rule of law.

I would like to think that Hong Kong passes the test after these six indicators have been properly considered. But that is of course not really for me to say but for the public to decide for itself. It is essential that the community does take a stand on this, for, as I have said earlier, public confidence in and respect for the rule of law is critical. If a jurisdiction passes this test, it will then have earned the respect that the rule of law needs. And where the rule of law does exist, it is undoubtedly a strength and becomes an institution that will have a long term future. This is by no means to say that it is not healthy to have concerns from time to time about the rule of law. I am not saying that, quite the contrary. Discussions and debates over such an important topic are healthy; after all, to adopt an old saying, the price for enjoying the rule of law is eternal vigilance. If fragility has the same meaning merely as concern, then strength and fragility can co-exist in tandem. If fragility has a more alarmist connotation, then one should best analyze the arguments and examine the facts objectively and dispassionately.

Finally, I profoundly thank the Bar for this opportunity to address you this evening. It is an emotional return to this great Hall. I am honoured to be back and I thank you all for that.

Fundamental Rights and State Security: Inseparable Allies

FRANÇOISE TULKENS

Former Judge and Vice-President of the European Court of Human Rights
Associate Member of the *Académie Royale de Belgique*

28 November 2016

I would like to begin by saying that I am very grateful to the Bar Council of England and Wales for this invitation. It is not only an honour but also a great pleasure to deliver the 10th International Rule of Law Lecture, especially in this prestigious venue which was of central importance to the drafting of the Magna Carta.

Today, for a variety of good and bad reasons, security issues have become or have again become pervasive at the national, European and international levels. This is obvious. But it is also clear that measures announced or adopted by Sates or organisations can raise unique and difficult questions in terms of respect of fundamental rights.

It seems to me more and more that the opposition between fundamental rights' requirements and security requirements is an appearance, an appearance the main function of which is to classify the positions of the various parties considered as enemies in separate camps. Yet, the opposition between the realists and the idealists, between the pragmatists and the laxists, between the responsible and the irresponsible, is radically false. Seeking security while ensuring respect – and an informed respect – for human rights is a guarantee of efficiency; conversely, security at the expense of human rights is an illusion. Ultimately, counter-terrorism is not conducted against the law but with the law.

In this perspective, I think that we should favour complex thought and avoid the false simplicity of obvious concepts. I will try to show that the obligation to fight terrorism is certainly an obligation but that this obligation is inseparable from the obligation to respect human rights. In fact we are faced with a double "categorical imperative, to borrow Immanuel Kant's analysis. I will then present the conditions and methods for reconciling these obligations in the jurisprudence of the European Court of Human Rights. But, to understand the importance and the stakes at play in the relationships between terrorism and human rights, I think that they have to be seen in the context of the requirements of the rule of law and I will start with that.

THE RULE OF LAW

In the current political debate, at least in continental Europe, the rule of law is repeatedly invoked, in very different contexts and situations, with the risk of becoming an "impossible" concept[1], even a "catch-all" concept (*un concept fourre-tout*). But, at the same time, and this is fairly new, some do no longer hesitate today to assert that it is a "matter of legal quibbling" (*une "argutie juridique"*) and to criticize the rule of law is becoming an acceptable, even trendy, posture. As a professor of constitutional law at the University of Paris 1 Panthéon-Sorbonne says, the rule of law is becoming blamed for all our problems. "The multiplication of terrorist attacks? It is the rule of law's fault! The insufficient action against terrorists? It is the rule of law's fault! (…) The flow of political refugees to Europe? It is the rule of law's fault! ..."[2].

The *rule of law*[3], what is it basically about? Without going into the genealogy and the eventful history of the discourse on the rule of law[4], I shall limit myself to recalling the *contours* / scope of the European model of the rule of law laid down in 1950 in the European Convention on Human Rights and enshrined in international[5] as well as in European Union law[6]. This model is characterised by two features: the right to the Law (*droit au droit*) and the right to justice (*droit au juge*). From a substantive viewpoint, the rule of law implies both a denial and an obligation. A denial, that of arbitrary actions and the abuse of power. An obligation, that is respect of human rights by all State bodies and public authorities. From a procedural viewpoint, the right to justice expresses the need for a judicial intervention and remedy, before an independent and impartial judge, who must be the "guardian of promises".

[1] M. Troper, "Le concept d'Etat de droit", *Droits*, no. 15, 1992, pp. 51 et seq.

[2] . D. Rousseau, "Mon plaidoyer pour l'Etat de droit", Tribune, *Libération*, 17 August 2016.

[3] *The Principle of the Rule of Law*, Report of the Committee on Legal Affairs and Human Rights of the Council of Europe Parliamentary Assembly (rapporteur: E. Jurgens), doc. 11343, 6 July 2007. See also T. Bingham, *The Rule of Law*, London, Penguin Book, 2011.

[4] See J. Chevalier, *L'Etat de droit*, Paris, Montchrestien, 4th edition, 2003; L. Heuschling, *L'Etat de droit, Rechstaat, Rule of Law*, Paris, Dalloz, 2002.

[5] See *L'Etat de droit en droit international*, Paris, Pedone, 2009.

[6] See D. Kochenov and L. Pech, "Renforcer le respect de l'Etat de droit dans l'UE: Regards critiques sur les nouveaux mécanismes proposés par la Commission et le Conseil", *Fondation Robert Schuman / Questions d'Europe*, no. 356, 11 May 2015.

As the vice-president of the French *Conseil d'Etat* Jean-Marc Sauvé rightly analyses, there is "a descriptive and tautological conception of the rule of law based on the idea that any State where law is a part of the State is a rule-of-law State. In this regard, one could say that a dictatorial regime is a rule-of-law State"[7]. That is a misunderstanding. A rule-of-law State is a State which complies with rules of law inspired by / based on respect for human rights and public freedoms.

The rule of law (*l'Etat de droit*) is therefore an essential democratic guarantee, even and particularly in the context of terrorism. It is radically different from the police state, which allows the Executive to "dictate the law" and to enforce it without controls. In this respect, state of emergency laws or draft laws which, for instance, allow the administrative authorities to assign people to house arrest without a court having to approve it or even to place someone in detention subject only to judicial review *a posteriori*, are highly problematic[8]. To detain people is not the task of the political authorities but of the judiciary. In an opinion issued on 17 December 2015 the French *Conseil d'Etat* clearly stated that, within the present constitutional framework, it was not possible, under the precautionary principle, to deprive persons flagged with fiche "S" (*personnes fichées "S"*) of their liberty on the basis of a suspicious conduct (and not activity)[9]. "In a country that lives in a prolonged state of emergency, and in which police operations progressively replace judicial power, a rapid and irreversible degradation of public institutions must be expected"[10]. In an opinion of 2 February 2016, the French *Conseil d'Etat* also recalled that a state of emergency, which is a state of crisis, cannot be renewed indefinitely[11].

Under the state of emergency introduced in Turkey following the failed *coup d'état* of 15 July 2016, large-scale purges are targeting all sectors of society (education, media, army, judiciary) and around 35,000 people have already been arrested according to the figures given by the ministry of Justice. The European Court of Human Rights has since then received a significant number of applications – more than 3,000 – lodged by persons

[7] J.-B. Jacquin, "Entretien avec J.-M. Sauvé", *Le Monde*, 18 novembre 2016.

[8] See, for instance, in France, Law No. 2016-731 of 3 July 2016 on organised crime and terrorism as well as Law no. 2016-987 of 21 July 2016 extending the state of emergency and strengthening counter-terrorism.

[9] *Avis sur la constitutionnalité et la compatibilité avec les engagements internationaux de la France de certaines mesures de prévention du risque de terrorisme*, adopted by the General Assembly of the Conseil d'Etat on 17 December 2015.

[10] G. Agamben, "De l'Etat de droit à l'Etat de sécurité" ("From the State of Law to the Security State"), *Le Monde*, 23 December 2015.

[11] *Avis sur un projet de loi prorogeant l'application de la loi n° 55-385 du 3 avril 1955 relative à l'état d'urgence*, adopted by the General Assembly of the Conseil d'Etat on 2 February 2016.

subjected to such measures. However, a first case, *Mercan v. Turkey*, which concerned the pre-trial detention of a judge who was dismissed from office a few days before the state of emergency which was proclaimed on 21 July 2016, was declared inadmissible by the Court on 8 November 2016 for failure to exhaust domestic remedies[12].

Let us now turn to my second and third points. The obligation to fight against terrorism and the obligation to respect human rights. In a seminal book that I am very indebted to, *Terrorism and the limitations of rights. The European Convention on Human Rights and the United States Constitution*[13], Stefan Sottiaux develops the idea of the paradoxical relations between terrorism and human rights[14]. I fully agree with him. It is indeed a real paradox and not a contradiction. A contradiction is like a knot, we untie it. But, in the case of a paradox, an attempt must be made to come to terms with it, while being aware of the complexity of the ensuing consequences, and to clarify it in the light of the requisite balance between its component parts. "Human rights law not only serves as a primary source of the State's responsibility to counter terrorism, but it also imposes the boundaries within which the State's response to terrorism must unfold"[15].

THE OBLIGATION TO FIGHT AGAINST TERRORISM

There are two reasons supporting this obligation[16] and I will address them in turn. They emanate from the idea that the European Convention on Human Rights does not operate in a vacuum but in a given political and social context.

The right to life

In the European Convention on Human Rights, the right directly concerned with terrorism is the right to life enshrined in Article 2. "Everyone's right to life shall be protected by the law", says the text. This right is the primary source of the obligation, for the States, to protect against terrorist acts. In other words, the lawfulness of action to combat terrorism finds its

[12] ECtHR, *Mercan v. Turkey* decision of 8 November 2016. Since the applicant's placement in pre-trial detention on 17 July was not a measure that had been adopted by legislative decree in the context of the state of emergency which was proclaimed on 21 July 2016, the Court considered that her argument that it was impossible for her to appeal against her placement in detention was unfounded.
[13] S. Sottiaux, *Terrorism and the Limitations of Rights. The European Convention on Human Rights and the United States Constitution*, Hart Publishing, Oxford / Portland, 2008.
[14] *Ibid.*, p. 2.
[15] *Ibid.*, p. 6.
[16] *Ibid.*, pp. 4-5.

justification in and is limited by the protection of the population's right to life and thereby places it outside any abstraction such as the *raison d'état* or national security[17].

The principle that States are required to take all reasonable steps to protect persons under their jurisdiction from life-endangering offences is a principle that is recognized in the European Court of Human Rights' jurisprudence. The *Osman v. the United Kingdom* judgment of 28 October 1998 extends its scope: "It is common ground that the State's obligation in this respect extends beyond its primary duty to secure the right to life by putting in place effective criminal-law provisions to deter the commission of offences against the person ... Article 2 of the Convention may also imply in certain well-defined circumstances a positive obligation on the authorities to take preventive operational measures to protect an individual whose life is at risk from the criminal acts of another individual"[18].

Therefore, when it comes to terrorism, the positive obligation for the States may be to put in place, in certain circumstances, effective prevention strategies. The Court will soon have to clarify the scope of the positive obligation of prevention in the case of *Tagayeva and Others v. Russia* which is currently pending and which concerns the hostage-taking at the Beslan school by a group of heavily armed terrorists arriving from neighbouring Ingushetia in September 2004. The applicants in this case complain of the lack of preventive measures in spite of the fact that intelligence services were aware of the risk of terrorist attacks and of the presence of terrorists within the area.

Furthermore, when counter-terrorism measures are justified, the State is required to organise them in such a way as to minimise the risk to life. The *Finogenov and Others v. Russia* judgment of 20 December 2011 which concerned the siege in October 2002 of the "Dubrovka" theatre in Moscow by Chechen separatists extends the *McCann and Others v. the United Kingdom* case-law[19]. The police had decided to overcome the terrorists and liberate the hostages using gas. The Court found that the use of gas against the terrorists during the theatre siege was justified and therefore held that there had been no substantive violation of the right to life concerning the decision to resolve the hostage crisis by force and use gas[20]. But it held that there had been a procedural violation of the right to life on account of the

17 Fr. Bernard, "La Cour européenne des droits de l'homme et la lutte contre le terrorisme", *Rev. trim. dr. h.*, 2016, p. 45.

18 ECtHR, *Osman v. the United Kingdom* judgment of 28 October 1998, § 115.

19 ECtHR, *McCann and Others v. the United Kingdom* du 27 septembre 1995, § 213.

20 ECtHR, *Finogenov and Others v. Russia* judgment of 20 December 2011.

inadequate planning and implementation of the rescue operation as well as of the lack of medical assistance to hostages and the ineffectiveness of the investigation into the allegations of the authorities' negligence[21].

In contrast, in the Grand Chamber judgment *Armani da Silva v. the United Kingdom* of 30 March 2016 concerning the fatal shooting of a Brazilian national mistakenly identified by the police as a suicide bomber, the Court found, having regard to the proceedings as a whole, that the authorities had not failed in their obligation to conduct an effective investigation[22].

Against this background, the assumption that the European Court of Human Rights prohibits democratic States from combating terrorism is deeply inaccurate. But, and this is quite another matter, States – and thus Governments – must take useful, appropriate and not illusory measures. Deprivation of nationality, which France wanted at some point to introduce in its Constitution, is to my mind a perfect counterexample. There is a case currently pending before the Court concerning deprivation of nationality for acts of terrorism, *A.S. v. France*, which was communicated to the Government on 5 October 2016 under Articles 3, 8, 14 and 34 of the Convention, as well as under Article 1 of Protocol No. 7 to the Convention[23].

Protection of the democratic system

There is a second reason why States have the obligation, under the European Convention on Human Rights, to combat terrorism. It arises from the threat posed by terrorism to a country's democratic system[24]. As the former President of the Supreme Court of Israel Aharon Barak puts it, " [i]f we do not protect democracy, democracy will not protect us [25]. Terrorist acts do not only affect individual human rights but their objective often includes also the neutralisation, even the destruction, of the entire political system. Furthermore, when they aim at provoking change through violence, terrorist methods are directly opposed to the democratic principles of democracy, namely the peaceful resolution of political conflicts by dialogue[26].

[21] *Ibid.*

[22] ECtHR (GC), *Armani da Silva v. the United Kingdom* judgment of 30 March 2016.

[23] Application no. 46240/15, *A.S. v. France*.

[24] S. Sottiaux, *Terrorism and the Limitations of Rights. The European Convention on Human Rights and the United States Constitution, op. cit.*, p. 5.

[25] A. Barak, "Human rights in terror – A judicial point of view", Seminar organised on the occasion of the opening of the judicial year of the European Court of Human Rights, Strasbourg, 29 January 2016.

[26] *Ibid.*, see ECtHR, *United Communist Party of Turkey and Others v. Turkey* judgment of 30 January 1998, § 57.

The Preamble to the European Convention on Human Rights is sendind out a strong message: "[F]undamental freedoms … are best maintained … by an effective political democracy …". European human rights law – and indeed international law – accordingly obliges States to ensure protection and preservation of their democratic system of government. Yet, a way of undermining democratic institutions and values is precisely to encourage Governments to combat terrorist violence by employing counter-terrorism measures which put them at risk. Things are closely connected. In other words, and to quote a famous formula used by the European Court, one cannot "undermin[e] or even destroy […] democracy on the ground of defending it"[27].

THE OBLIGATION TO RESPECT HUMAN RIGHTS

While States cannot fail to fulfil their obligation to adopt adequate and effective counter-terrorism measures, they cannot either fail to fulfil their obligation to respect human rights, which they undertook to observe when signing and ratifying the various European and international instruments for the protection of fundamental rights to which they are parties. Starting with the 1948 Universal Declaration of Human Rights and the 1950 European Convention on Human Rights up to the Charter of Fundamental Rights of the European Union adopted in 2000 and which became binding with the entry into force of the Lisbon Treaty in 2009.

The State's obligation to respect human rights is based on two main reasons that share in common the need to ensure the legitimacy of interventions and thus their effectiveness.

Abuse of power / authority

Human rights provide guarantees against abuse of power, which directly undermines the legitimacy of the fight against terrorism. Yet, abuse of power, under the form of slippages or drifts, which constitute serious violations of human rights, are real and not imaginary. I shall take recent examples in cases lodged before the European Court of Human Rights in 2012, 2014 and 2016.

Following the 11 September 2001 attacks, several countries in Europe provided assistance to the United States for the rendition to and the secret detention by the CIA, on their territory, of terror suspects prior to their transfer to the US Naval Base in Guantanamo Bay, which enabled to subtract

[27] ECtHR, *Klass and Others v. Germany* judgment of 6 September 1978, § 49.

them from the rules of law. In the *El-Masri* Grand Chamber judgment of 13 December 2012, "the former Yugoslav Republic of Macedonia" had assisted the CIA in capturing a German citizen who was held in secret for several months in a hotel in Skopje. The Court found a violation of Article 3 of the Convention on account of the ill-treatment to which the applicant had been subjected while being held in the hotel and at Skopje Airport, which amounted to torture[28]. The Court also stressed – and this is important – that victims and the general public have a right to the truth[29].

The same situation occurred in Poland, at a CIA "black site", with so-called "enhanced interrogation techniques" and "unauthorised" interrogation methods including, among other things, mock executions, "waterboard technique", stress positions, confinement in a box and threats of abuse against the applicants' families. In the *Al Nashiri v. Poland* judgment of 24 July 2014 the Court held that there had been a violation of Article 2 and Article 3 of the Convention taken together with Article 1 of Protocol No. 6 concerning the abolition of the death penalty, finding that Poland had enabled the CIA to transfer the applicant to the jurisdiction of a military commission in Guantanamo and thus exposed him to a foreseeable serious risk that he could be subjected to the death penalty following his trial[30].

Following the *Nasr and Ghali v. Italy* judgment of 23 February 2016, which concerned the abduction by CIA agents, with the cooperation of Italian officials, of a political refugee, and his subsequent transfer to Egypt where he was held in secret for several months in extreme conditions, where the Court also found a violation of Article 3 of the Convention[31], cases are still pending before the Court today, involving Romania and Lithuania, in which the Court held hearings on 29 June 2016[32]. Both applications concern alleged renditions of persons suspected of terrorist acts to CIA secret detention sites at which, according to the applicants' submissions, interrogation methods amounting to torture were used. The United Nations Special Rapporteur on the promotion and protection of human rights and fundamental freedoms while countering terrorism was, among others, invited to submit written comments as a third party and to take part in the hearings.

[28] ECtHR (GC), *El-Masri v. "the former Yugoslav Republic of Macedonia"* of 13 December 2012, § 223.
[29] *Ibid.*, § 191.
[30] ECtHR, *Al Nashiri v. Poland* judgment of 24 July 2014, §§ 578-579.
[31] ECtHR, *Nasr and Ghali v. Italy* judgment of 23 February 2016, §§ 284-291.
[32] Applications *Al Nashiri v. Romania* (no. 33234/12) and *Abu Zubaydah v. Lithuania* (no. 46454/11).

The risk of arbitrariness

When the obligation to combat terrorism requires special prevention and prosecution strategies or measures, such measures must be carried out in a way fully in line with the principles of the rule of law in order to ensure control over the relevance and the necessity of the counter-terrorism measures and avoid the risk of arbitrariness.

What is arbitrariness? In a nutshell, arbitrariness is the ability to decide free from any rule. It targets decisions which are outside a normative framework and refers to a power without any control and accountability. The existence of a principle of legality– substantive legality and procedural legality – is the main guarantee against arbitrary government decisions[33].

Numerous judgments of the European Court are eminently indicative of the pressing need for such a control. In the Grand Chamber judgment *Del Río Prada v. Spain* of 21 October 2013, the applicant, who was serving a prison sentence of 30 years for being a member of a terrorist organisation, alleged that what she considered to be the retroactive application of a departure from the case-law by the Supreme Court after she had been convicted, had extended her detention by almost nine years, in violation of Article 7 of the Convention. The Court recalled that "[t]he guarantee enshrined in Article 7 … should be construed and applied, as follows from its object and purpose, in such a way as to provide effective safeguards against arbitrary prosecution, conviction and punishment"[34]. In this respect, it noted "that the *Audiencia Nacional* used the new method of application of remissions of sentence for work done in detention introduced by the "Parot doctrine" rather than the method in use at the time of the commission of the offences and the applicant's conviction, thus depriving her of any real prospect of benefiting from the remissions of sentence to which she was nevertheless entitled in accordance with the law. … This change in the system for applying remissions of sentence was the result of the Supreme Court's departure from previous case-law, as opposed to a change in legislation"[35]. In this connection, "while the Court accepts that the States are free to determine their own criminal policy, for example by increasing the penalties applicable to criminal offences …, they must comply with the requirements of Article 7 in doing so … On this point, the Court reiterates that Article 7 of the Convention unconditionally prohibits the retrospective

[33] See J. Portier, "La notion d'arbitraire dans la jurisprudence de la Cour européenne des droits de l'homme", *Les cahiers de la justice*, no. 2016/3, pp. 521 et seq.

[34] ECtHR (GC), *Del Río Prada v. Spain* judgment of 21 October 2013, § 77.

[35] *Ibid.*, §§ 111-112.

application of the criminal law where it is to an accused's disadvantage ..."[36].

Deprivations of liberty are the place *par excellence* where there is a risk of arbitrariness. The *Sher and Others v. the United Kingdom* judgment of 20 October 2015, which involved the right to liberty and security, however problematic to my mind, is nevertheless interesting in so far as it contextualises the guarantees against the risk of arbitrariness. The case concerned the arrest and detention of three Pakistani nationals in the context of a counterterrorism operation. The applicants were detained for 13 days, before ultimately being released without charge. During that period they were brought twice before a court with warrants for their further detention being granted. They were then taken into immigration detention and had since voluntarily returned to Pakistan. They complained in particular about the hearings on requests for prolongation of their detention. In this case the Court found no violation of Article 5 § 4 of the Convention[37]. Reiterating that terrorism fell into a special category, it held that this provision could not be used to prevent the use of a closed hearing or to place disproportionate difficulties in the way of police authorities in taking effective measures to counter terrorism. In the applicants' case, the threat of an imminent terrorist attack and national security considerations had justified restrictions on the applicants' right to adversarial proceedings concerning the warrants for their further detention. Moreover, there had been sufficient safeguards against the risk of arbitrariness in respect of the proceedings for warrants of further detention, in the form of a legal framework setting out clear and detailed procedural rules.

RECONCILING THE OBLIGATIONS

For long, but especially since the years 2000, the European Court of Human Rights has been repeatedly called upon to decide cases involving counter-terrorism measures adopted by States[38]. The Court considers that the obligation of States to combat terrorism may, in certain circumstances and under certain conditions, justify restrictions on rights recognised in the Convention. But in accordance with the principles of necessity and proportionality, that is to say that such limitations must not go beyond what is strictly necessary in order to fulfil the obligation of protection

[36] *Ibid.*, §§ 116-117.

[37] ECtHR, *Sher and Others v. the United Kingdom* judgment of 20 October 2015, §§ 150-157.

[38] Fr. Bernard, "La Cour européenne des droits de l'homme et la lutte contre le terrorisme", *op. cit.*

and that the impossibility to resort to other, less harmful to the rights and freedoms and equally effective means, is established. However, the State's positive obligation may not call into question the absolute nature of non-derogable right and, notably, the prohibition of torture and inhuman or degrading treatment.

Let us examine that more closely because here a careful analysis of the jurisprudence of the European Court of Human Rights, which goes beyond prejudices and slogans, is required.

Absolute rights

As we all know, the European Convention on Human Rights contains certain rights which are absolute, non-derogable, and which are not subject to exceptions, even in time of war or other public emergency threatening the life of the nation. As far as the prohibition of torture and inhuman or degrading treatment is concerned, despite pressure from the States Parties, the Court has always stood firm: "Even in the most difficult circumstances, such as the fight against terrorism and organised crime, the Convention prohibits in absolute terms torture and inhuman or degrading treatment or punishment"[39]. Why? It is quite simply the universal value of human dignity, which everyone is to enjoy respect for and which distinguishes us precisely from terrorist barbarity. Abandoning it or renouncing to it is simply a step backwards for civilisation (*recul de civilisation*).

In the *Saadi v. Italy* Grand Chamber judgment of 28 February 2008, the Court ruled against the expulsion of a terrorist suspect to Tunisia, where the applicant was likely to be subjected to torture or inhuman or degrading treatment[40]. The Court thereby confirmed the absolute nature of Article 3 of the Convention which entails, incidentally, a wider guarantee than the one laid down in Articles 32 and 33 of the 1951 United Nations Convention on the Status of Refugees. The Court noted in particular that "States face immense difficulties in modern times in protecting their communities from terrorist violence ... It cannot therefore underestimate the scale of the danger of terrorism today and the threat it presents to the community. That must not, however, call into question the absolute nature of Article 3 ..."[41].

This principled position was reiterated in the *A. and Others v. the United Kingdom* Grand Chamber judgment of 19 February 2009: "The Court

[39] ECtHR (GC), *Selmouni v. France* judgment of 28 July 1999, § 95; ECtHR (GC), *Labita v. Italy* judgment of 6 April 2000, § 119; ECtHR (GC), *Ramirez Sanchez v. France* judgment of 4 July 2006, § 115. See also ECtHR (GC), *Gäfgen v. Germany* judgment of 1 June 2010, § 87.
[40] ECtHR (GC), *Saadi v. Italy* judgment of 28 February 2008, § 127.
[41] *Ibid.*, § 137.

is acutely conscious of the difficulties faced by States in protecting their populations from terrorist violence. This makes it all the more important to stress that Article 3 enshrines one of the most fundamental values of democratic societies. Unlike most of the substantive clauses of the Convention and of Protocols Nos. 1 and 4, Article 3 makes no provision for exceptions and no derogation from it is permissible under Article 15 § 2 notwithstanding the existence of a public emergency threatening the life of the nation. Even in the most difficult of circumstances, such as the fight against terrorism, and irrespective of the conduct of the person concerned, the Convention prohibits in absolute terms torture and inhuman or degrading treatment and punishment ..."[42]. Let us note that in the present judgment, in which the European Court of Human Rights, like the House of Lords, found that the derogatory measures had been disproportionate in that they had discriminated unjustifiably between nationals and non-nationals[43], is particularly interesting in so far as it provides an overview of the European Court's case-law concerning the right of derogation under Article 15 of the Convention.

The *Trabelsi v. Belgium* judgment of 4 September 2014 concerns another situation. In this case the Court ruled against the extradition of the applicant to the United States where he was being prosecuted on charges of terrorist offences, for which he was liable to an irreducible life sentence, that is to say a sentence with no possibility of a review. The Court considered that in view of the gravity of the terrorist offences with which the applicant stood charged and the fact that a sentence could only be imposed after the trial court had taken into consideration all relevant mitigating and aggravating factors, a discretionary life sentence would not be grossly disproportionate[44]. It found, however, that the US authorities had at no point provided any concrete assurance that the applicant would be spared an irreducible life sentence. The Court also noted that, while US legislation provided various possibilities for reducing life sentences (including the Presidential pardon system), which gave the applicant some "prospect of release", it did not lay down any procedure amounting to a mechanism for reviewing such sentences for the purposes of Article 3 of the Convention. Therefore, the life imprisonment to which the applicant might be sentenced could not be described as reducible, which meant that his extradition to the United States had amounted to a violation of Article 3[45].

42 ECtHR (GC), *A. and Others v. the United Kingdom* judgment of 19 February 2009, § 139.
43 *Ibid.*, § 190.
44 ECtHR, *Trabelsi v. Belgium* judgment of 4 September 2014, § 127.
45 *Ibid.*, §§ 136-139.

I know that there is resistance in the United Kingdom against the *Vinter and Others* Grand Chamber judgment of 9 July 2013 concerning whole-life sentences and the subsequent judgments in the cases of Öcalan v. Turkey (no. 2) of 18 March 2014 and *Murray v. the Netherlands* (Grand Chamber) of 26 April 2016. Soon we will see if in the case of *Hutchinson v. the United Kingdom,* currently pending before the Grand Chamber, the Court will confirm its case-law. Moreover, the Grand Chamber will be holding a hearing on 11 January 2017 in the case of *Harkins v. the United Kingdom,* which concerns an extradition order to the United States of America where the applicant is facing a mandatory life sentence in prison without parole.

By contrast, the *Othman (Abu Qatada) v. the United Kingdom* judgment of 17 January 2012 reaches a different conclusion. With regard to Article 3 of the Convention, the Court noted that, in accordance with its well-established case-law, the applicant could not be deported to Jordan if there were a real risk that he would be tortured or subjected to inhuman or degrading treatment. Yet, the reports of United Nations bodies and human rights organisations showed that the Jordanian General Intelligence Directorate routinely used torture against suspected Islamist terrorists and that no protection against that was provided by the courts or any other body in Jordan. The Court therefore had to decide whether the diplomatic assurances obtained by the UK authorities from the Jordanian Government were sufficient to protect the applicant. The Court found that the agreement between the two Governments was specific and comprehensive. The assurances were given in good faith by a Government whose bilateral relations with the United Kingdom had, historically, been strong. In addition, the assurances would be monitored by an independent human rights organisation in Jordan, which would have full access to the applicant in prison. The Court therefore held that there would be no risk of ill-treatment and no violation of Article 3 if the applicant were deported to Jordan.

Authorised limitations, restrictions or interferences

All the other Convention rights may, under certain conditions, be subjected either to exceptions, limitations or restrictions, or to State interferences.

I will not address here Article 15 of the Convention which affords to the Governments of the States parties, in exceptional circumstances, that is to say in time of war or other public emergency threatening the life of the nation, the possibility of derogating, in a temporary, limited and supervised manner, from their obligation to secure certain rights and freedoms under the Convention, to the extent strictly required by the exigencies of the situation. This provision which, in some way, puts the Convention rights "on the back burner" (*en veilleuse*), is governed by very strict procedural and substantive conditions, which are intended to prevent abuses. Its use is relatively limited since, as shown by Athanasia Petropoulou, the Convention system allows States sufficient flexibility to respond effectively to the terrorist threat without resorting to the derogation provided for by Article 15[46]. I shall therefore address two rights, among others, which are most likely to be affected by counter-terrorism measures: the right to a fair trial and the right to respect for private life.

The right to a fair trial

Article 6 of the Convention guarantees the right to a fair trial. Counter-terrorism measures are a major test for many aspects of this right, such as for instance the right to silence[47], the presumption of innocence or the rights of the defence[48]. In addition, the means employed, such as anonymous witness testimony, undercover techniques, the use of informers, special methods of investigation or trials held before special courts[49] create as many situations where there is a risk. The search for immediate effectiveness – which is not easy matter – may pave the way for abuses and arbitrariness. This is the reason why the Convention emphasises the pre-eminence of the law and the role of the judge in the protection of human rights[50].

In the *Othman (Abu Qatada) v. the United Kingdom* judgment of 17 January 2012 which I have already mentioned earlier with regard to Article 3 of the Convention, the second question before the Court was that of whether the applicant would be at real risk of a flagrantly unfair trial if he were deported to Jordan, where he was wanted on terrorism charges. The European Court agreed with the Court of Appeal that the use of evidence obtained by torture during a criminal trial would amount to a flagrant denial of justice, in violation of Article 6 of the Convention[51]. Allowing a criminal court to rely on torture evidence would indeed legitimise the torture of witnesses and suspects pre-trial. Moreover, torture evidence was

46 A. Petropoulou, *Liberté et sécurité: les mesures antiterroristes et la Cour européenne des droits de l'homme*, Paris, Pedone, 2014, p. 492.

47 ECtHR, *Heaney and McGuinness v. Ireland* judgment of 21 December 2000.

48 ECtHR (GC), *Salduz v. Turkey* judgment of 27 November 2008.

49 ECtHR, *Incal v. Turkey* judgment of 9 June 1998.

50 See Consultative Council of European Judges, *Opinion no.° (2006) Opinion No. 8 (2006) of the Consultative Council of European Judges (CCJE) for the attention of the Committee of Ministers of the Council of Europe on "the role of judges in the protection of the rule of law and human rights in the context of terrorism"*, doc. CCJE(2006)3, adopted by the CCJE at its 7th meeting, Strasbourg, 10 November 2006.

51 ECtHR, *Othman (Abu Qatada) v. the United Kingdom* judgment of 17 January 2012, §§ 263-267.

unreliable, because a person being tortured would say anything to make it stop. The Court also agreed with the UK Special Immigration Appeals Commission that there was a high probability that the incriminating evidence would be admitted at the applicant's retrial and that it would be of considerable, perhaps decisive, importance. In the absence of any assurance by Jordan that the torture evidence would not be used against the applicant, the Court therefore concluded that his deportation to Jordan to be retried would give rise to a flagrant denial of justice in violation of Article 6.

The *El Haski v. Belgium* judgment of 25 September 2012 concerned the Belgian courts refusal to exclude as evidence statements taken in Morocco where there was a real risk that they had been obtained by torture[52]. Moreover, on the basis of several reports issued by the United Nations and non-governmental organisations, the European Court noted that at the relevant time the Moroccan judicial system did not offer real guarantees of independent, impartial and serious examination of allegations of torture or inhuman or degrading treatment. Article 6 of the Convention – the right to a fair trial – therefore required the domestic courts not to admit them as evidence without first making sure they had not been obtained by torture. However, in rejecting the applicant's request to exclude the statements, the Court of Appeal simply noted that he had provided no "concrete proof" capable of shedding "reasonable doubt" on the evidence, which was clearly insufficient.

By contrast, in the *McKevitt and Campbell v. the United Kingdom* decision of 6 September 2016, the Court unanimously declared the application inadmissible under Article 6 §§ 1 et 3 (d) of the Convention. In regard to the evidence of an FBI agent who had not been made available in court for questioning, it found in particular that the judge had fully considered the need for appropriate safeguards given the witness's absence, namely that the applicants had had an adequate opportunity to challenge the agent's evidence with their own and that the judge had had due regard to the appropriate considerations when deciding what weight he could attach to the evidence of an absent witness. In light of this, the Court found that the national court's findings could not be said to have been arbitrary or unreasonable[53]. The applicants had not demonstrated that their trial was unfair, and the Court dismissed their applications. This echoes the idea

[52] ECtHR, *El Haski v. Belgium* judgment of 25 September 2012.
[53] ECtHR, *Mc Kevitt and Campbell v. the United Kingdom* decision of 6 September 2016, § 68.

that procedural guarantees can, in certain cases, compensate for obstacles faced by the defence and prevent the risk of abuse.

Lastly, the rights of the defence are an essential aspect of the right to a fair trial. For those who think that the European Court of Human Rights exercises a unilateral control or that is is naïve, laxist and cut-off from reality, the *Ibrahim and Others v. the United Kingdom* Grand Chamber judgment of 13 September 2016 constitutes another counterexample. It concerns delayed access to lawyers during police questioning of the 21st July 2005 London bombers. The Court accepted that the police had temporarily delayed access to a lawyer of those suspected, because there had been an exceptionally serious and imminent threat to public safety, namely the risk of a terrorist attacks[54]. We can certainly regret this judgment and I do. The Court's reasoning must be read, in all its shades and waves. On the one hand, the Court recalled that "[t]he general requirements of fairness contained in Article 6 apply to all criminal proceedings, irrespective of the type of offence in issue. There can be no question of watering down fair trial rights for the sole reason that the individuals in question are suspected of involvement in terrorism. In these challenging times, the Court considers that it is of the utmost importance that the Contracting Parties demonstrate their commitment to human rights and the rule of law by ensuring respect for, *inter alia,* the minimum guarantees of Article 6 of the Convention"[55]. On the other hand, "when determining whether the proceedings as a whole have been fair the weight of the public interest in the investigation and punishment of the particular offence in issue may be taken into consideration ... Moreover, Article 6 should not be applied in such a manner as to put disproportionate difficulties in the way of the police authorities in taking effective measures to counter terrorism or other serious crimes in discharge of their duty under Articles 2, 3 and 5 § 1 of the Convention to protect the right to life and the right to bodily security of members of the public"[56]. Finally, as a sort of concession, the Court admits that "public interest concerns cannot justify measures which extinguish the very essence of an applicant's defence rights ..."[57].

My main concern is the following one. Is the obligation of the police to discharge its duty under Articles 2, 3 and 5 § 1 of the Convention to protect the right to life and to bodily security of members of the public radically prevented by the presence of a lawyer? Can one infer that the assistance of

[54] ECtHR (GC), *Ibrahim and Others v. the United Kingdom* judgment of 13 September 2016.
[55] *Ibid.*, § 252.
[56] *Ibid.*
[57] *Ibid.*

a lawyer will put "disproportionate difficulties" in the way of the police authorities in taking effective measures to counter terrorism? "The specific status of lawyers gives them a central position in the administration of justice as intermediaries between the public and the courts. They therefore play a key role in ensuring that the courts, whose mission is fundamental in a State based on the rule of law, enjoy public confidence ..."[58]. Furthermore, what is "the very essence of an applicant's defence rights" if it is not the assistance, in due time, of a lawyer?

The right to respect for private life

I shall now turn to the so-called rights with relative protection, where interferences in the exercise of the rights and freedoms are authorised under certain conditions. The right to thought, conscience and religion (Article 9 of the European Convention on Human Rights), freedom of expression (Article 10), freedom of assembly and association (Article 11) are rights that are very often involved in the case of terrorism. I am thinking, for example, to hate speech[59] or apology of terrorism.

I will however restrict myself to the right of respect for private and family life guaranteed by Article 8 of the Convention. We are facing the critical importance of intelligence activities in the fight against terrorism (identification and interception of communications, observation, a.s.o.) because the ability of States' security services to prevent terrorist attacks quite often depends on the quality of information they have available. States' interferences in the exercise of this right are subject to a three-fold condition (foreseen by the law, pursuing a legitimate aim and necessary in a democratic society) and, therefore, a rigorous methodology is necessary during the concrete examination of each case.

In this respect, interferences must be provided for by the law, which corresponds to a basic democratic requirement. States cannot act on the basis of vague legal provisions. Under the guise of combating terrorism, no other forms of crime can be included. "Dead-weight effect" (*l'effet d'aubaine*) refers to this extension of the scope of counter-terrorism measures/strategies beyond their area of origin[60]. So, for instance, in the

58 See the joint partly dissenting, partly concurring opinion of Judges Sajó and Laffranque annexed to the *Ibrahim and Others v. the United Kingdom* judgment, at § 21.

59 See Fr. Tulkens, "When to say is to do. Freedom of expression and hate speech in the case-law of the European Court of Human Rights", *Freedom of expression. Essays in Honour of Nicolas Bratza*, Oisterwijk, Wolf Legal Publishers, 2012, pp. 279- et seq.

60 O. De Schutter, "La Convention européenne des droits de l'homme à l'épreuve de la lutte contre le terrorisme", in E. Bribosia and A. Weyembergh (eds), *Lutte contre le terrorisme et droits fondamentaux*, Brussels, Bruylant, 2002, pp. 90 et seq.

Gillan and Quinton v. the United Kingdom judgment of 12 January 2010, which concerned the police power under sections 44-47 of the Terrorism Act 2000 to stop and search individuals without reasonable suspicion of wrongdoing, the Court found that some provisions of the 2000 Act were neither sufficiently circumscribed nor subject to adequate legal safeguards against abuse, so that the interference with Article 8 of the Convention had not been in accordance with the law.[61]. The application in the case of *Sylvie Beghal v. the United Kingdom* which was lodged before the European Court of Human Rights on 14 January 2016 and communicated to the UK Government on 22 April 2016 raises the same question in the context of Schedule 7 to the Terrorism Act 2000 which, without prior authorisation, empowers police, immigration officers and designated customs officers to stop, examine and search passengers at ports, airports and international rail terminals.

Interferences must also pursue a legitimate aim which, in the case of terrorism, will most often be national security and the protection of the rights and freedom of others. These aims must be clearly defined. However, the Court will rarely question the evaluation by the States, which are thus entitled a wide margin of appreciation as to the existence of a situation affecting national security.

Lastly, interferences must be necessary in a democratic society to achieve the legitimate aims pursued. To this end, interferences will be considered to be necessary if they answer a pressing social need and if they are proportionate to the aims pursued. The reasons adduced by the national authorities to justify the interference are relevant and pertinent. So, for instance, in the *Blaj v. Romania* judgment of 8 April 2014, the tapping of the applicant's telephone conversations had been ordered on account of suspicion of passive corruption and authorised by a court order[62]. Moreover, "for a measure to be regarded as proportionate and as necessary in a democratic society, the possibility of recourse to an alternative measure that would cause less damage to the fundamental right in issue whilst fulfilling the same aim must be ruled out ..."[63]. Ultimately, interferences with the right to respect for private life enshrined in Article 8 of the Convention are, in some cases, accepted only on the grounds that the State compensated for the limitation on the applicant's right in question[64]. In any event, if "the final evaluation of whether the interference

[61] ECtHR, *Gillan and Quinton v. the United Kingdom* judgment of 12 January 2010, § 87.

[62] ECtHR, *Blaj v. Romania* judgment of 8 April 2014.

[63] ECtHR (GC), *Nada v. Switzerland* judgment of 12 September 2012, § 183.

[64] ECtHR, *Klass v. Germany* judgment of 6 September 1978, §§ 46 et s.

is necessary remains subject to review by the Court for conformity with the requirements of the Convention ... [a] margin of appreciation must be left to the competent national authorities in this connection. The breadth of this margin varies and depends on a number of factors including the nature of the Convention right in issue, its importance for the individual, the nature of the interference and the object pursued by the interference ..."[65].

Regarding intelligence issues, mass surveillance – which is sometimes referred to as general and not targeted surveillance – is a constant temptation for many States which view human rights as an obstacle to public safety[66]. I am aware that on 18 November 2016 the United Kingdom Parliament has passed the Investigatory Powers Bill which is the most extreme surveillance law in its history. However, some express concern that, by allowing indiscriminate surveillance of persons who are not suspected of terrorist activities, laws may aggravate social tensions because they are likely to create a dangerous environment in which all individuals are regarded as potential suspects. "The State is poisoning itself", as Antoine Garapon puts it.

This is the type of counter-terrorism measure that endangers fundamental rights and is counter-productive, diverting resources that might prevent terrorist attacks. Already in 2015, the Report of the Committee on Legal Affairs and Human Rights of the Council of Europe Parliamentary Assembly noted that "[m]ass surveillance d[id] not appear to have contributed to the prevention of terrorist attacks, contrary to earlier assertions made by senior intelligence officials. Instead, resources that might prevent attacks are diverted to mass surveillance, leaving potentially dangerous persons free to act". The Assembly therefore called for the collection and analysis of personal data (including so-called metadata) without consent only following "a court order granted on the basis of reasonable suspicion". It also recommended for a better judicial and parliamentary control of intelligence services and for the adoption of an "intelligence codex" defining mutual obligations that secret services could opt into. It lastly called for "credible, effective protection" for whistle-blowers exposing unlawful surveillance[67].

[65] ECtHR (GC), *Nada v. Switzerland* judgment of 12 September 2012, § 184.

[66] See Fr. Dubuisson, "La Cour européenne des droits de l'homme et la surveillance de masse", *Rev. trim. dr. h.*, 2016, pp. 855 et seq.

[67] *Mass surveillance*, Report of the Committee on Legal Affairs and Human Rights of the Council of Europe Parliamentary Assembly (rapporteur: P. Omtzigt), doc. 13734, 18 March 2015.

As far as surveillance is concerned, the law must be precise and clear as to the nature of the charged or suspected activities of persons who may be subjected to surveillance. It must set out strict limits on the duration of the operations, as well as rules on the use, storage and destruction of data obtained during those operations. Persons subjected to surveillance operations must have an effective remedy in order to contest the validity of the measures applied to them, as well as the decisions on the use and storage of the data concerning them. In addition, the law should also increase the accountability and transparency of the intelligence services, including vis-à-vis Parliament. Lastly, large-scale surveillance must also conform to the strict tests of necessity and proportionality in order to be compatible with Article 8 of the European Convention on Human Rights. This is the thrust of the *Szabo and Vissy v. Hungary* judgment of 12 January 2016[68] which, on this point, draws inter alia on two recent judgments of the Court of Justice of the European Union[69].

CONCLUSION

International human rights law does not prevent States from taking measures in order to protect their citizens from the threat of terrorism. The European Convention on Human Rights is not a "suicidal" convention. But the Executive cannot be left in a position of power with no effective control. Restrictions on individual freedoms must be limited to what is absolutely necessary, they must be temporary and subject to a regular assessment process. They must be targeted with sufficient precision and must not encompass other phenomena, maybe even categories of undesirable persons.

I am thinking here of migrants and refugees. "Overly-restrictive migration policies introduced because of terrorism concerns are not justified and may in fact be damaging to State security," warned the United Nations Special Rapporteur on counter-terrorism and human rights before the UN General Assembly on 21 October 2016. Presenting his last report on the impact of counter-terrorism on the human rights of migrants and refugees, Ben Emmerson showed that "while there is no evidence that migration leads to increased terrorist activity, migration policies that

[68] . ECtHR, *Szabo and Vissy v. Hungary* judgment of 12 January 2016, §§ 69-70.

[69] . CJEU (GC), *Digital Rights Ireland Ltd v. Minister for Communications, Marine and Natural Resources and Others and Kärntner Landesregierung and Others* judgment of 8 April 2014, joined cases C-293/12 et C-594/12; CJEU (GC), *Maximillian Schrems v. Data Protection Commissioner* judgment of 6 October 2015, case C-362/14.

are restrictive or that violate human rights may in fact create conditions conducive to terrorism"[70].

The rule of law cannot accept snap legislation and never can fear be a valid reason for violating fundamental human rights. While in Hobbes political philosophy the State is "that which effectively brings an end to fear", in the Security State, "this schema is reversed: the State is durably grounded in fear and must, at all cost, maintain it, because it draws from it its essential function and its legitimacy"[71]. In this respect, I regret that the political authorities do not further play or do not longer play their prominent role of peacekeeper. Within a complex reality such as terrorism, Governments must play a pedagogical and not a demagogic role.

In a recent book, *The Crisis of the European Union: A Response*, Habermas expands on what he calls "the realistic utopia of human rights"[72]. "The origin of human rights in the moral notion of human dignity explains the explosive political force of a concrete utopia"[73]. Far from taking an idealistic but noncommittal stance or adopting the cynical pose of the so-called realists, human rights constitute a realistic utopia insofar as they anchor the ideal of a just society in the institutions of democratic States themselves. This utopia is very simply the right to think of the future and to think of it differently.

[70] Report of the Special Rapporteur on the promotion and protection of human rights and fundamental freedoms while countering terrorism, doc. A/71/384, 13 September 2016.
[71] G. Agamben, "De l'Etat de droit à l'Etat de sécurité", *op. cit.*
[72] J. Habermas, *The Crisis of the European Union: A Response*, Ciaran Cronin (tr.), Cambridge, Polity Press, 2012, pp. 71 et seq.
[73] *Ibid.*